CALIFORNIA

EVIDENCE CODE

2026 EDITION

I0894652

League Publishing Inc.

ISBN: 979-8-90113-564-8
www.californiaevidencecode.com

EDITORIAL NOTE

This book compiles the statutory provisions of the California Evidence Code present at the time of publication (August 2026), specifically Divisions 1 through 11, as enacted by the Legislature of the State of California. The statutory text is presented in its official form and organized for ease of reference. No commentary, analysis, or interpretation is intended.

This book includes the foundational provisions and construction of the Evidence Code, including statutory definitions, general evidentiary principles, judicial notice, burdens of proof, presumptions and inferences, and the rules governing the admissibility and exclusion of evidence. It further covers the qualifications and competency of witnesses, expert testimony, scientific evidence, privileges, hearsay rules and their exceptions, as well as the authentication and proof of writings.

Particular attention is given to statutory provisions governing evidentiary procedures in judicial proceedings, including the evaluation of evidence, credibility of witnesses, mediation confidentiality, opinion testimony, evidentiary privileges, and documentary evidence. The contents reflect the statutory framework used by California courts in determining the admissibility, reliability, and legal effect of evidence presented in civil and criminal proceedings.

This compilation also includes provisions relating to specialized evidentiary matters such as interpreters and translators, hypnosis of witnesses, immunity of news media personnel from contempt citations, mediation confidentiality, character evidence, scientific evidence, hearsay exceptions, and official writings affecting property. The organization follows the statutory structure established under the California Evidence Code.

The California Evidence Code is a work of the public domain. This publication does not claim authorship of the statutory text. The material has been compiled, arranged, and formatted solely for usability and reference purposes.

This compilation was prepared by Jeremy J. Salvador, who served exclusively in an editorial and organizational capacity. Responsibility for the substance and content of the law remains with the Legislature of the State of California. Users are advised to consult relevant case law, court rules, administrative regulations, and other legal authorities when applying the Code to specific legal situations.

The Code is organized in accordance with its official statutory structure, particularly reflecting Division 1: Preliminary Provisions and Construction [Sections 1 - 12], Division 2: Words and Phrases Defined [Sections 100 - 260], Division 3: General Provisions [Sections 300 - 413], Division 4: Judicial Notice [Sections 450 - 460], Division 5: Burden of Proof; Burden of Producing Evidence; Presumptions and Inferences [Sections 500 - 670], Division 6: Witnesses [Sections

700 - 795], Division 7: Opinion Testimony and Scientific Evidence [Sections 800 - 870], Division 8: Privileges [Sections 900 - 1070], Division 9: Evidence Affected or Excluded by Extrinsic Policies [Sections 1100 - 1162], Division 10: Hearsay Evidence [Sections 1200 - 1390], and Division 11: Writings [Sections 1400 - 1605], including their respective chapters and provisions as enacted.

CONTENTS

CONTENTS

DIVISION 1: PRELIMINARY PROVISIONS AND CONSTRUCTION

DIVISION 1 ENACTED BY STATS. 1965, CH. 299.
SECTION 1 - 12

1. This code shall be known as the Evidence Code.[1]

2. The rule of the common law, that statutes in derogation thereof are to be strictly construed, has no application to this code. This code establishes the law of this state respecting the subject to which it relates, and its provisions are to be liberally construed with a view to effecting its objects and promoting justice.[1]

3. If any provision or clause of this code or application thereof to any person or circumstances is held invalid, such invalidity shall not affect other provisions or applications of the code which can be given effect without the invalid provision or application, and to this end the provisions of this code are declared to be severable.[1]

4. Unless the provision or context otherwise requires, these preliminary provisions and rules of construction shall govern the construction of this code.[1]

5. Division, chapter, article, and section headings do not in any manner affect the scope, meaning, or intent of the provisions of this code.[1]

6. Whenever any reference is made to any portion of this code or of any other statute, such reference shall apply to all amendments and additions heretofore or hereafter made.[1]

7. Unless otherwise expressly stated:
(a) "Division" means a division of this code.
(b) "Chapter" means a chapter of the division in which that term occurs.
(c) "Article" means an article of the chapter in which that term occurs.
(d) "Section" means a section of this code.
(e) "Subdivision" means a subdivision of the section in which that term occurs.
(f) "Paragraph" means a paragraph of the subdivision in which that term occurs.[1]

8. The present tense includes the past and future tenses; and the future, the present.[1]

9. The masculine gender includes the feminine and neuter.[1]

10. The singular number includes the plural; and the plural, the singular.[1]

11. "Shall" is mandatory and "may" is permissive.[1]

12. (a) This code shall become operative on January 1, 1967, and shall govern proceedings in actions brought on or after that date and, except as provided in subdivision (b), further proceedings in actions pending on that date.
(b) Subject to subdivision (c), a trial commenced before January 1, 1967, shall not be governed by this code. For the purpose of this subdivision:
(1) A trial is commenced when the first witness is sworn or the first exhibit is admitted into evidence and is terminated when the issue upon

which such evidence is received is submitted to the trier of fact. A new trial, or a separate trial of a different issue, commenced on or after January 1, 1967, shall be governed by this code.

(2) If an appeal is taken from a ruling made at a trial commenced before January 1, 1967, the appellate court shall apply the law applicable at the time of the commencement of the trial.

(c) The provisions of Division 8 (commencing with Section 900) relating to privileges shall govern any claim of privilege made after December 31, 1966.[1]

DIVISION 2: WORDS AND PHRASES DEFINED

DIVISION 2 ENACTED BY STATS. 1965, CH. 299.
SECTION 100 - 260

100. Unless the provision or context otherwise requires, these definitions govern the construction of this code.[1]

105. "Action" includes a civil action and a criminal action.[1]

110. "Burden of producing evidence" means the obligation of a party to introduce evidence sufficient to avoid a ruling against him on the issue.[1]

115. "Burden of proof" means the obligation of a party to establish by evidence a requisite degree of belief concerning a fact in the mind of the trier of fact or the court. The burden of proof may require a party to raise a reasonable doubt concerning the existence or nonexistence of a fact or that he establish the existence or nonexistence of a fact by a preponderance of the evidence, by clear and convincing proof, or by proof beyond a reasonable doubt.
Except as otherwise provided by law, the burden of proof requires proof by a preponderance of the evidence.[1]

120. "Civil action" includes civil proceedings.[1]

125. "Conduct" includes all active and passive behavior, both verbal and nonverbal.[1]

130. "Criminal action" includes criminal proceedings.[1]

135. "Declarant" is a person who makes a statement.[1]

140. "Evidence" means testimony, writings, material objects, or other things presented to the senses that are offered to prove the existence or nonexistence of a fact.[1]

145. "The hearing" means the hearing at which a question under this code arises, and not some earlier or later hearing.[1]

150. "Hearsay evidence" is defined in Section 1200.[1]

160. "Law" includes constitutional, statutory, and decisional law.[1]

165. "Oath" includes affirmation or declaration under penalty of perjury.[1]

170. "Perceive" means to acquire knowledge through one's senses.[1]

175. "Person" includes a natural person, firm, association, organization, partnership, business trust, corporation, limited liability company, or public entity.[54]

177. "Dependent person" means a person, regardless of whether the person lives independently, who has a physical or mental impairment that substantially restricts his or her ability to carry out normal activities or to protect his or her rights, including, but not limited to, persons who have physical or developmental disabilities or whose physical or mental abilities have significantly diminished because of age. "Dependent person" includes any person who is admitted as an inpatient to a 24-hour health facility, as defined in Sections 1250, 1250.2, and 1250.3 of the Health and Safety Code.[142]

180. "Personal property" includes money, goods, chattels, things in action, and evidences of debt.[1]

185. "Property" includes both real and personal property.[1]

190. "Proof" is the establishment by evidence of a requisite degree of belief concerning a fact in the mind of the trier of fact or the court.[1]

195. "Public employee" means an officer, agent, or employee of a public entity.[1]

200. "Public entity" includes a nation, state, county, city and county, city, district, public authority, public agency, or any other political subdivision or public corporation, whether foreign or domestic.[1]

205. "Real property" includes lands, tenements, and hereditaments.[1]

210. "Relevant evidence" means evidence, including evidence relevant to the credibility of a witness or hearsay declarant, having any tendency in reason to prove or disprove any disputed fact that is of consequence to the determination of the action.[1]

215. "Spouse" includes "registered domestic partner," as required by Section 297.5 of the Family Code.[126]

220. "State" means the State of California, unless applied to the different parts of the United States. In the latter case, it includes any state, district, commonwealth, territory, or insular possession of the United States.[1]

225. "Statement" means (a) oral or written verbal expression or (b) nonverbal conduct of a person intended by him as a substitute for oral or written verbal expression.[1]

230. "Statute" includes a treaty and a constitutional provision.[1]

235. "Trier of fact" includes (a) the jury and (b) the court when the court is trying an issue of fact other than one relating to the admissibility of evidence.[1]

240. (a) Except as otherwise provided in subdivision (b), "unavailable as a witness" means that the declarant is any of the following:

(1) Exempted or precluded on the ground of privilege from testifying concerning the matter to which his or her statement is relevant.

(2) Disqualified from testifying to the matter.

(3) Dead or unable to attend or to testify at the hearing because of then-existing physical or mental illness or infirmity.

(4) Absent from the hearing and the court is unable to compel his or her attendance by its process.

(5) Absent from the hearing and the proponent of his or her statement has exercised reasonable diligence but has been unable to procure his or her attendance by the court's process.

(6) Persistent in refusing to testify concerning the subject matter of the declarant's statement despite having been found in contempt for refusal to testify.

(b) A declarant is not unavailable as a witness if the exemption, preclusion, disqualification, death, inability, or absence of the declarant was brought about by the procurement or wrongdoing of the proponent of his or her statement for the purpose of preventing the declarant from attending or testifying.

(c) Expert testimony that establishes that physical or mental trauma resulting from an alleged crime has caused harm to a witness of sufficient severity that the witness is physically unable to testify or is unable to testify without suffering substantial trauma may constitute a sufficient showing of unavailability pursuant to paragraph (3) of subdivision (a). As used in this section, the term "expert" means a physician and surgeon, including a psychiatrist, or any person described by subdivision (b), (c), or (e) of Section 1010.

The introduction of evidence to establish the unavailability of a witness under this subdivision shall not be deemed procurement of unavailability, in absence of proof to the contrary.[110]

250. "Writing" means handwriting, typewriting, printing, photostating, photographing, photocopying, transmitting by electronic mail or facsimile, and every other means of recording upon any tangible thing, any form of communication or representation, including letters, words, pictures, sounds, or symbols, or combinations thereof, and any record thereby created, regardless of the manner in which the record has been stored.[89]

255. "Original" means the writing itself or any counterpart intended to have the same effect by a person executing or issuing it. An "original" of a photograph includes the negative or any print therefrom. If data are stored in a computer or similar device, any printout or other output readable by sight, shown to reflect the data accurately, is an "original."[17]

260. A "duplicate" is a counterpart produced by the same impression as the original, or from the same matrix, or by means of photography, including enlargements and miniatures, or by mechanical or electronic rerecording, or by chemical reproduction, or by other equivalent technique which accurately reproduces the original.[17]

DIVISION 3: GENERAL PROVISIONS

DIVISION 3 ENACTED BY STATS. 1965, CH. 299.
SECTION 300 - 413

Chapter 1: Applicability of Code

Chapter 1 enacted by Stats. 1965, Ch. 299.

300. Except as otherwise provided by statute, this code applies in every action before the Supreme Court or a court of appeal or superior court, including proceedings in such actions conducted by a referee, court commissioner, or similar officer, but does not apply in grand jury proceedings.[82]

Chapter 2: Province of Court and Jury

Chapter 2 enacted by Stats. 1965, Ch. 299.

310. (a) All questions of law (including but not limited to questions concerning the construction of statutes and other writings, the admissibility of evidence, and other rules of evidence) are to be decided by the court. Determination of issues of fact preliminary to the admission of evidence are to be decided by the court as provided in Article 2 (commencing with Section 400) of Chapter 4.
(b) Determination of the law of an organization of nations or of the law of a foreign nation or a public entity in a foreign nation is a question of law to be determined in the manner provided in Division 4 (commencing with Section 450).[1]

311. If the law of an organization of nations, a foreign nation or a state other than this state, or a public entity in a foreign nation or a state other than this state, is applicable and such law cannot be determined, the court may, as the ends of justice require, either:
(a) Apply the law of this state if the court can do so consistently with the Constitution of the United States and the Constitution of this state; or
(b) Dismiss the action without prejudice or, in the case of a reviewing court, remand the case to the trial court with directions to dismiss the action without prejudice.[1]

312. Except as otherwise provided by law, where the trial is by jury:
(a) All questions of fact are to be decided by the jury.
(b) Subject to the control of the court, the jury is to determine the effect and value of the evidence addressed to it, including the credibility of witnesses and hearsay declarants.[1]

Chapter 3: Order of Proof

Chapter 3 enacted by Stats. 1965, Ch. 299.

320. Except as otherwise provided by law, the court in its discretion shall regulate the order of proof.[1]

Chapter 4: Admitting and Excluding Evidence

Chapter 4 enacted by Stats. 1965, Ch. 299.

Article 1: General Provisions

Article 1 enacted by Stats. 1965, Ch. 299.

350. No evidence is admissible except relevant evidence.[1]

351. Except as otherwise provided by statute, all relevant evidence is admissible.[1]

351.1. (a) Notwithstanding any other provision of law, the results of a polygraph examination, the opinion of a polygraph examiner, or any reference to an offer to take, failure to take, or taking of a polygraph examination, shall not be admitted into evidence in any criminal proceeding, including pretrial and post-conviction motions and hearings, or in any trial or hearing of a juvenile for a criminal offense, whether heard in juvenile or adult court, unless all parties stipulate to the admission of such results.
(b) Nothing in this section is intended to exclude from evidence statements made during a polygraph examination which are otherwise admissible.[30]

351.2. (a) In a civil action for personal injury or wrongful death, evidence of a person's immigration status shall not be admitted into evidence, nor shall discovery into a person's immigration status be permitted.
(b) This section does not affect the standards of relevance, admissibility, or discovery prescribed by Section 3339 of the Civil Code, Section 7285 of the Government Code, Section 24000 of the Health and Safety Code, and Section 1171.5 of the Labor Code.[133]

351.3. (a) In a civil action not governed by Section 351.2, evidence of a person's immigration status shall not be disclosed in open court by a party or their attorney unless the judge presiding over the matter first determines that the evidence is admissible in an in camera hearing requested by the party seeking disclosure of the person's immigration status.
(b) This section does not do any of the following:
(1) Apply to cases in which a person's immigration status is necessary to prove an element of a claim or an affirmative defense.
(2) Impact otherwise applicable laws governing the relevance of immigration status to liability or the standards applicable to inquiries regarding immigration status in discovery or proceedings in a civil action, including Section 3339 of the Civil Code, Section 7285 of the Government Code, Section 24000 of the Health and Safety Code, and Section 1171.5 of the Labor Code.
(3) Prohibit a person or their attorney from voluntarily revealing the person's immigration status to the court.[164]

351.4. (a) In a criminal action, evidence of a person's immigration status shall not be disclosed in open court by a party or their attorney unless the judge presiding over the matter first determines that the evidence is admissible in an in camera hearing requested by the party seeking disclosure of the person's immigration status.
(b) This section does not do any of the following:
(1) Apply to cases in which a person's immigration status is necessary to prove an element of an offense or an affirmative defense.
(2) Limit discovery in a criminal action.
(3) Prohibit a person or their attorney from voluntarily revealing the person's immigration status to the court.[165]

352. The court in its discretion may exclude evidence if its probative value is substantially outweighed by the proba-

bility that its admission will (a) necessitate undue consumption of time or (b) create substantial danger of undue prejudice, of confusing the issues, or of misleading the jury.[1]

352.1. In any criminal proceeding under Section 261, 262, or 264.1, subdivision (d) of Section 286, or subdivision (d) of Section 287 of, or former Section 288a of, the Penal Code, or in any criminal proceeding under subdivision (c) of Section 286 or subdivision (c) of Section 287 of, or former Section 288a of, the Penal Code in which the defendant is alleged to have compelled the participation of the victim by force, violence, duress, menace, or threat of great bodily harm, the district attorney may, upon written motion with notice to the defendant or the defendant's attorney, if he or she is represented by an attorney, within a reasonable time prior to any hearing, move to exclude from evidence the current address and telephone number of any victim at the hearing.

The court may order that evidence of the victim's current address and telephone number be excluded from any hearings conducted pursuant to the criminal proceeding if the court finds that the probative value of the evidence is outweighed by the creation of substantial danger to the victim.

Nothing in this section shall abridge or limit the defendant's right to discover or investigate the information.[146]

352.2. (a) In any criminal proceeding where a party seeks to admit as evidence a form of creative expression, the court, while balancing the probative value of that evidence against the substantial danger of undue prejudice under Section 352, shall consider, in addition to the factors listed in Section 352, that: (1) the probative value of such expression for its literal truth or as a truthful narrative is minimal unless that expression is created near in time to the charged crime or crimes, bears a sufficient level of similarity to the charged crime or crimes, or includes factual detail not otherwise publicly available; and (2) undue prejudice includes, but is not limited to, the possibility that the trier of fact will, in violation of Section 1101, treat the expression as evidence of the defendant's propensity for violence or general criminal disposition as well as the possibility that the evidence will explicitly or implicitly inject racial bias into the proceedings.

(b) If proffered and relevant to the issues in the case, the court shall consider the following as well as any additional relevant evidence offered by either party:

(1) Credible testimony on the genre of creative expression as to the social or cultural context, rules, conventions, and artistic techniques of the expression.

(2) Experimental or social science research demonstrating that the introduction of a particular type of expression explicitly or implicitly introduces racial bias into the proceedings.

(3) Evidence to rebut such research or testimony.

(c) For purposes of this section, "creative expression" means the expression or application of creativity or imagination in the production or arrangement of forms, sounds, words, movements, or symbols, including, but not limited to, music, dance, performance art, visual art, poetry, literature, film, and other such objects or media.

(d) The question of the admissibility of a form of creative expression shall be heard in limine and determined by the court, outside the presence and hearing of the jury, pursuant to Section 402. The court shall state on the record its ruling and its reasons therefor.[169]

353. A verdict or finding shall not be set aside, nor shall the judgment or decision based thereon be reversed, by reason of the erroneous admission of evidence unless:
(a) There appears of record an objection to or a motion to exclude or to strike the evidence that was timely made and so stated as to make clear the specific ground of the objection or motion; and
(b) The court which passes upon the effect of the error or errors is of the opinion that the admitted evidence should have been excluded on the ground stated and that the error or errors complained of resulted in a miscarriage of justice.[1]

354. A verdict or finding shall not be set aside, nor shall the judgment or decision based thereon be reversed, by reason of the erroneous exclusion of evidence unless the court which passes upon the effect of the error or errors is of the opinion that the error or errors complained of resulted in a miscarriage of justice and it appears of record that:
(a) The substance, purpose, and relevance of the excluded evidence was made known to the court by the questions asked, an offer of proof, or by any other means;
(b) The rulings of the court made compliance with subdivision (a) futile; or
(c) The evidence was sought by questions asked during cross-examination or recross-examination.[1]

355. When evidence is admissible as to one party or for one purpose and is inadmissible as to another party or for another purpose, the court upon request shall restrict the evidence to its proper scope and instruct the jury accordingly.[1]

356. Where part of an act, declaration, conversation, or writing is given in evidence by one party, the whole on the same subject may be inquired into by an adverse party; when a letter is read, the answer may be given; and when a detached act, declaration, conversation, or writing is given in evidence, any other act, declaration, conversation, or writing which is necessary to make it understood may also be given in evidence.[1]

Article 2: Preliminary Determinations on Admissibility of Evidence
Article 2 enacted by Stats. 1965, Ch. 299.

400. As used in this article, "preliminary fact" means a fact upon the existence or nonexistence of which depends the admissibility or inadmissibility of evidence. The phrase "the admissibility or inadmissibility of evidence" includes the qualification or disqualification of a person to be a witness and the existence or nonexistence of a privilege.[1]

401. As used in this article, "proffered evidence" means evidence, the admissibility or inadmissibility of which is dependent upon the existence or nonexistence of a preliminary fact.[1]

402. (a) When the existence of a preliminary fact is disputed, its existence or nonexistence shall be determined as provided in this article.
(b) The court may hear and determine

the question of the admissibility of evidence out of the presence or hearing of the jury; but in a criminal action, the court shall hear and determine the question of the admissibility of a confession or admission of the defendant out of the presence and hearing of the jury if any party so requests.

(c) A ruling on the admissibility of evidence implies whatever finding of fact is prerequisite thereto; a separate or formal finding is unnecessary unless required by statute.[1]

403. (a) The proponent of the proffered evidence has the burden of producing evidence as to the existence of the preliminary fact, and the proffered evidence is inadmissible unless the court finds that there is evidence sufficient to sustain a finding of the existence of the preliminary fact, when:

(1) The relevance of the proffered evidence depends on the existence of the preliminary fact;

(2) The preliminary fact is the personal knowledge of a witness concerning the subject matter of his testimony;

(3) The preliminary fact is the authenticity of a writing; or

(4) The proffered evidence is of a statement or other conduct of a particular person and the preliminary fact is whether that person made the statement or so conducted himself.

(b) Subject to Section 702, the court may admit conditionally the proffered evidence under this section, subject to evidence of the preliminary fact being supplied later in the course of the trial.

(c) If the court admits the proffered evidence under this section, the court:

(1) May, and on request shall, instruct the jury to determine whether the preliminary fact exists and to disregard the proffered evidence unless the jury finds that the preliminary fact does exist.

(2) Shall instruct the jury to disregard the proffered evidence if the court subsequently determines that a jury could not reasonably find that the preliminary fact exists.[1]

404. Whenever the proffered evidence is claimed to be privileged under Section 940, the person claiming the privilege has the burden of showing that the proffered evidence might tend to incriminate him; and the proffered evidence is inadmissible unless it clearly appears to the court that the proffered evidence cannot possibly have a tendency to incriminate the person claiming the privilege.[1]

405. With respect to preliminary fact determinations not governed by Section 403 or 404:

(a) When the existence of a preliminary fact is disputed, the court shall indicate which party has the burden of producing evidence and the burden of proof on the issue as implied by the rule of law under which the question arises. The court shall determine the existence or nonexistence of the preliminary fact and shall admit or exclude the proffered evidence as required by the rule of law under which the question arises.

(b) If a preliminary fact is also a fact in issue in the action:

(1) The jury shall not be informed of the court's determination as to the existence or nonexistence of the preliminary fact.

(2) If the proffered evidence is admitted, the jury shall not be instructed to disregard the evidence if its determination of the fact differs from the

court's determination of the preliminary fact.[1]

406. This article does not limit the right of a party to introduce before the trier of fact evidence relevant to weight or credibility.[1]

Chapter 5: Weight of Evidence Generally

Chapter 5 enacted by Stats. 1965, Ch. 299.

410. As used in this chapter, "direct evidence" means evidence that directly proves a fact, without an inference or presumption, and which in itself, if true, conclusively establishes that fact.[1]

411. Except where additional evidence is required by statute, the direct evidence of one witness who is entitled to full credit is sufficient for proof of any fact.[1]

412. If weaker and less satisfactory evidence is offered when it was within the power of the party to produce stronger and more satisfactory evidence, the evidence offered should be viewed with distrust.[1]

413. In determining what inferences to draw from the evidence or facts in the case against a party, the trier of fact may consider, among other things, the party's failure to explain or to deny by his testimony such evidence or facts in the case against him, or his willful suppression of evidence relating thereto, if such be the case.[1]

DIVISION 4:
JUDICIAL NOTICE

DIVISION 4 ENACTED BY STATS. 1965, CH. 299.
SECTION 450 - 460

450. Judicial notice may not be taken of any matter unless authorized or required by law.[1]

451. Judicial notice shall be taken of the following:
(a) The decisional, constitutional, and public statutory law of this state and of the United States and the provisions of any charter described in Section 3, 4, or 5 of Article XI of the California Constitution.
(b) Any matter made a subject of judicial notice by Section 11343.6, 11344.6, or 18576 of the Government Code or by Section 1507 of Title 44 of the United States Code.
(c) Rules of professional conduct for members of the bar adopted pursuant to Section 6076 of the Business and Professions Code and rules of practice and procedure for the courts of this state adopted by the Judicial Council.
(d) Rules of pleading, practice, and procedure prescribed by the United States Supreme Court, such as the Rules of the United States Supreme Court, the Federal Rules of Civil Procedure, the Federal Rules of Criminal Procedure, the Admiralty Rules, the Rules of the Court of Claims, the Rules of the Customs Court, and the General Orders and Forms in Bankruptcy.
(e) The true signification of all English words and phrases and of all legal expressions.
(f) Facts and propositions of generalized knowledge that are so universally known that they cannot reasonably be the subject of dispute.[35]

452. Judicial notice may be taken of the following matters to the extent that they are not embraced within Section 451:
(a) The decisional, constitutional, and statutory law of any state of the United States and the resolutions and private acts of the Congress of the United States and of the Legislature of this state.
(b) Regulations and legislative enactments issued by or under the authority of the United States or any public entity in the United States.
(c) Official acts of the legislative, executive, and judicial departments of the United States and of any state of the United States.
(d) Records of (1) any court of this state or (2) any court of record of the United States or of any state of the United States.
(e) Rules of court of (1) any court of this state or (2) any court of record of the United States or of any state of the United States.
(f) The law of an organization of nations and of foreign nations and public entities in foreign nations.
(g) Facts and propositions that are of such common knowledge within the territorial jurisdiction of the court that they cannot reasonably be the subject of dispute.
(h) Facts and propositions that are not reasonably subject to dispute and are capable of immediate and accurate determination by resort to sources of reasonably indisputable accuracy.[1]

452.5. (a) The official acts and records specified in subdivisions (c) and (d) of Section 452 include any computer-generated official court records, as specified by the Judicial Council, that relate to criminal convictions, when the record is certified by a clerk of the superior court pursuant to Section 69844.5 of the Government Code at the time of computer entry.

(b) (1) An official record of conviction certified in accordance with subdivision (a) of Section 1530, or an electronically digitized copy thereof, is admissible under Section 1280 to prove the commission, attempted commission, or solicitation of a criminal offense, prior conviction, service of a prison term, or other act, condition, or event recorded by the record.

(2) For purposes of this subdivision, "electronically digitized copy" means a copy that is made by scanning, photographing, or otherwise exactly reproducing a document, is stored or maintained in a digitized format, and meets either of the following requirements:

(A) The copy bears an electronic signature or watermark unique to the entity responsible for certifying the document.

(B) The copied document is an official record of conviction, certified in accordance with subdivision (a) of Section 1530, that is transmitted by the clerk of the superior court in a manner showing that the copy was prepared and transmitted by that clerk of the superior court. A seal, signature, or other indicia of the court shall constitute adequate showing.[139]

453. The trial court shall take judicial notice of any matter specified in Section 452 if a party requests it and:

(a) Gives each adverse party sufficient notice of the request, through the pleadings or otherwise, to enable such adverse party to prepare to meet the request; and

(b) Furnishes the court with sufficient information to enable it to take judicial notice of the matter.[1]

454. (a) In determining the propriety of taking judicial notice of a matter, or the tenor thereof:

(1) Any source of pertinent information, including the advice of persons learned in the subject matter, may be consulted or used, whether or not furnished by a party.

(2) Exclusionary rules of evidence do not apply except for Section 352 and the rules of privilege.

(b) Where the subject of judicial notice is the law of an organization of nations, a foreign nation, or a public entity in a foreign nation and the court resorts to the advice of persons learned in the subject matter, such advice, if not received in open court, shall be in writing.[1]

455. With respect to any matter specified in Section 452 or in subdivision (f) of Section 451 that is of substantial consequence to the determination of the action:

(a) If the trial court has been requested to take or has taken or proposes to take judicial notice of such matter, the court shall afford each party reasonable opportunity, before the jury is instructed or before the cause is submitted for decision by the court, to present to the court information relevant to (1) the propriety of taking judicial notice of the matter and (2) the tenor of the matter to be noticed.

(b) If the trial court resorts to any source of information not received in open court, including the advice of persons learned in the subject matter, such information and its source shall be made a part of the record in the action and the court shall afford each party reasonable opportunity to meet such information before judicial notice of the matter may be taken.[1]

456. If the trial court denies a request to take judicial notice of any matter, the court shall at the earliest practicable time so advise the parties and indicate for the record that it has denied the request.[1]

457. If a matter judicially noticed is a matter which would otherwise have been for determination by the jury, the trial court may, and upon request shall, instruct the jury to accept as a fact the matter so noticed.[1]

458. The failure or refusal of the trial court to take judicial notice of a matter, or to instruct the jury with respect to the matter, does not preclude the trial court in subsequent proceedings in the action from taking judicial notice of the matter in accordance with the procedure specified in this division.[1]

459. (a) The reviewing court shall take judicial notice of (1) each matter properly noticed by the trial court and (2) each matter that the trial court was required to notice under Section 451 or 453. The reviewing court may take judicial notice of any matter specified in Section 452. The reviewing court may take judicial notice of a matter in a tenor different from that noticed by the trial court.

(b) In determining the propriety of taking judicial notice of a matter, or the tenor thereof, the reviewing court has the same power as the trial court under Section 454.

(c) When taking judicial notice under this section of a matter specified in Section 452 or in subdivision (f) of Section 451 that is of substantial consequence to the determination of the action, the reviewing court shall comply with the provisions of subdivision (a) of Section 455 if the matter was not theretofore judicially noticed in the action.

(d) In determining the propriety of taking judicial notice of a matter specified in Section 452 or in subdivision (f) of Section 451 that is of substantial consequence to the determination of the action, or the tenor thereof, if the reviewing court resorts to any source of information not received in open court or not included in the record of the action, including the advice of persons learned in the subject matter, the reviewing court shall afford each party reasonable opportunity to meet such information before judicial notice of the matter may be taken.[1]

460. Where the advice of persons learned in the subject matter is required in order to enable the court to take judicial notice of a matter, the court on its own motion or on motion of any party may appoint one or more such persons to provide such advice. If the court determines to appoint such a person, he shall be appointed and compensated in the manner provided in Article 2 (commencing with Section 730) of Chapter 3 of Division 6.[1]

DIVISION 5: BURDEN OF PROOF; BURDEN OF PRODUCING EVIDENCE; PRESUMPTIONS AND INFERENCES

DIVISION 5 ENACTED BY STATS. 1965, CH. 299
SECTION 500 - 670

Chapter 1: Burden of Proof

Chapter 1 enacted by Stats. 1965, Ch. 299.

Article 1: General

Article 1 enacted by Stats. 1965, Ch. 299.

500. Except as otherwise provided by law, a party has the burden of proof as to each fact the existence or nonexistence of which is essential to the claim for relief or defense that he is asserting.[1]

501. Insofar as any statute, except Section 522, assigns the burden of proof in a criminal action, such statute is subject to Penal Code Section 1096.[1]

502. The court on all proper occasions shall instruct the jury as to which party bears the burden of proof on each issue and as to whether that burden requires that a party raise a reasonable doubt concerning the existence or nonexistence of a fact or that he establish the existence or nonexistence of a fact by a preponderance of the evidence, by clear and convincing proof, or by proof beyond a reasonable doubt.[1]

Article 2: Burden of Proof on Specific Issues

Article 2 enacted by Stats. 1965, Ch. 299.

520. The party claiming that a person is guilty of crime or wrongdoing has the burden of proof on that issue.[1]

521. The party claiming that a person did not exercise a requisite degree of care has the burden of proof on that issue.[1]

522. The party claiming that any person, including himself, is or was insane has the burden of proof on that issue.[1]

523. In any action where the state is a party, regardless of who is the moving party, where (a) the boundary of land patented or otherwise granted by the state is in dispute, or (b) the validity of any state patent or grant dated prior to 1950 is in dispute, the state shall have the burden of proof on all issues relating to the historic locations of rivers, streams, and other water bodies and the authority of the state in issuing the patent or grant.

This section is not intended to nor shall it be construed to supersede existing statutes governing disputes where the state is a party and regarding title to real property.[53]

524. (a) Notwithstanding any other provision of law, in a civil proceeding to which the State Board of Equalization is a party, that board shall have the burden of proof by clear and convincing evidence in sustaining its assertion of a penalty for intent to evade or fraud against a taxpayer, with respect to any factual issue relevant to ascertaining the liability of a taxpayer.

(b) Nothing in this section shall be construed to override any requirement for a taxpayer to substantiate any item

on a return or claim filed with the State Board of Equalization.
(c) Nothing in this section shall subject a taxpayer to unreasonable search or access to records in violation of the United States Constitution, the California Constitution, or any other law.
(d) For purposes of this section, "taxpayer" includes a person on whom fees administered by the State Board of Equalization are imposed.[108]

Chapter 2: Burden of Producing Evidence

Chapter 2 enacted by Stats. 1965, Ch. 299.

550. (a) The burden of producing evidence as to a particular fact is on the party against whom a finding on that fact would be required in the absence of further evidence.
(b) The burden of producing evidence as to a particular fact is initially on the party with the burden of proof as to that fact.[1]

Chapter 3: Presumptions and Inferences

Chapter 3 enacted by Stats. 1965, Ch. 299.

Article 1: General

Article 1 enacted by Stats. 1965, Ch. 299.

600. (a) A presumption is an assumption of fact that the law requires to be made from another fact or group of facts found or otherwise established in the action. A presumption is not evidence.
(b) An inference is a deduction of fact that may logically and reasonably be drawn from another fact or group of facts found or otherwise established in the action.[1]

601. A presumption is either conclusive or rebuttable. Every rebuttable presumption is either (a) a presumption affecting the burden of producing evidence or (b) a presumption affecting the burden of proof.[1]

602. A statute providing that a fact or group of facts is prima facie evidence of another fact establishes a rebuttable presumption.[1]

603. A presumption affecting the burden of producing evidence is a presumption established to implement no public policy other than to facilitate the determination of the particular action in which the presumption is applied.[1]

604. The effect of a presumption affecting the burden of producing evidence is to require the trier of fact to assume the existence of the presumed fact unless and until evidence is introduced which would support a finding of its nonexistence, in which case the trier of fact shall determine the existence or nonexistence of the presumed fact from the evidence and without regard to the presumption. Nothing in this section shall be construed to prevent the drawing of any inference that may be appropriate.[1]

605. A presumption affecting the burden of proof is a presumption established to implement some public policy other than to facilitate the determination of the particular action in which the presumption is applied, such as the policy in favor of establishment of a parent and child relationship, the validity of marriage, the stability of titles to property, or the security of those who entrust themselves or their property to

the administration of others.[16]

606. The effect of a presumption affecting the burden of proof is to impose upon the party against whom it operates the burden of proof as to the nonexistence of the presumed fact.[1]

607. When a presumption affecting the burden of proof operates in a criminal action to establish presumptively any fact that is essential to the defendant's guilt, the presumption operates only if the facts that give rise to the presumption have been found or otherwise established beyond a reasonable doubt and, in such case, the defendant need only raise a reasonable doubt as to the existence of the presumed fact.[1]

Article 2: Conclusive Presumptions
Article 2 enacted by Stats. 1965, Ch. 299.

620. The presumptions established by this article, and all other presumptions declared by law to be conclusive, are conclusive presumptions.[1]

622. The facts recited in a written instrument are conclusively presumed to be true as between the parties thereto, or their successors in interest; but this rule does not apply to the recital of a consideration.[1]

623. Whenever a party has, by his own statement or conduct, intentionally and deliberately led another to believe a particular thing true and to act upon such belief, he is not, in any litigation arising out of such statement or conduct, permitted to contradict it.[1]

624. A tenant is not permitted to deny the title of his landlord at the time of the commencement of the relation.[1]

Article 3: Presumptions Affecting the Burden of Producing Evidence
Article 3 enacted by Stats. 1965, Ch. 299.

630. The presumptions established by this article, and all other rebuttable presumptions established by law that fall within the criteria of Section 603, are presumptions affecting the burden of producing evidence.[1]

631. Money delivered by one to another is presumed to have been due to the latter.[1]

632. A thing delivered by one to another is presumed to have belonged to the latter.[1]

633. An obligation delivered up to the debtor is presumed to have been paid.[1]

634. A person in possession of an order on himself for the payment of money, or delivery of a thing, is presumed to have paid the money or delivered the thing accordingly.[1]

635. An obligation possessed by the creditor is presumed not to have been paid.[1]

636. The payment of earlier rent or installments is presumed from a receipt for later rent or installments.[1]

637. The things which a person possesses are presumed to be owned by him.[1]

638. A person who exercises acts of ownership over property is presumed to be the owner of it.[1]

639. A judgment, when not conclusive, is presumed to correctly determine or set forth the rights of the parties, but there is no presumption that the facts essential to the judgment have been correctly determined.[1]

640. A writing is presumed to have been truly dated.[1]

641. A letter correctly addressed and properly mailed is presumed to have been received in the ordinary course of mail.[1]

642. A trustee or other person, whose duty it was to convey real property to a particular person, is presumed to have actually conveyed to him when such presumption is necessary to perfect title of such person or his successor in interest.[1]

643. A deed or will or other writing purporting to create, terminate, or affect an interest in real or personal property is presumed to be authentic if it:
(a) Is at least 30 years old;
(b) Is in such condition as to create no suspicion concerning its authenticity;
(c) Was kept, or if found was found, in a place where such writing, if authentic, would be likely to be kept or found; and
(d) Has been generally acted upon as authentic by persons having an interest in the matter.[1]

644. A book, purporting to be printed or published by public authority, is presumed to have been so printed or published.[1]

645. A book, purporting to contain reports of cases adjudged in the tribunals of the state or nation where the book is published, is presumed to contain correct reports of such cases.[1]

645.1. Printed materials, purporting to be a particular newspaper or periodical, are presumed to be that newspaper or periodical if regularly issued at average intervals not exceeding three months.[36]

646. (a) As used in this section, "defendant" includes any party against whom the res ipsa loquitur presumption operates.
(b) The judicial doctrine of res ipsa loquitur is a presumption affecting the burden of producing evidence.
(c) If the evidence, or facts otherwise established, would support a res ipsa loquitur presumption and the defendant has introduced evidence which would support a finding that he was not negligent or that any negligence on his part was not a proximate cause of the occurrence, the court may, and upon request shall, instruct the jury to the effect that:
(1) If the facts which would give rise to res ipsa loquitur presumption are found or otherwise established, the jury may draw the inference from such facts that a proximate cause of the occurrence was some negligent conduct on the part of the defendant; and
(2) The jury shall not find that a proximate cause of the occurrence was some negligent conduct on the part of the defendant unless the jury believes, after weighing all the evidence in the case and drawing such inferences therefrom as the jury believes are warranted, that it is more probable than not that the occurrence was caused by some negligent conduct on the part of the defendant.[9]

647. The return of a process server registered pursuant to Chapter 16 (commencing with Section 22350) of

Division 8 of the Business and Professions Code upon process or notice establishes a presumption, affecting the burden of producing evidence, of the facts stated in the return.[20]

Article 4: Presumptions Affecting the Burden of Proof
Article 4 enacted by Stats. 1965, Ch. 299.

660. The presumptions established by this article, and all other rebuttable presumptions established by law that fall within the criteria of Section 605, are presumptions affecting the burden of proof.[1]

662. The owner of the legal title to property is presumed to be the owner of the full beneficial title. This presumption may be rebutted only by clear and convincing proof.[1]

663. A ceremonial marriage is presumed to be valid.[1]

664. It is presumed that official duty has been regularly performed. This presumption does not apply on an issue as to the lawfulness of an arrest if it is found or otherwise established that the arrest was made without a warrant.[1]

665. A person is presumed to intend the ordinary consequences of his voluntary act. This presumption is inapplicable in a criminal action to establish the specific intent of the defendant where specific intent is an element of the crime charged.[1]

666. Any court of this state or the United States, or any court of general jurisdiction in any other state or nation, or any judge of such a court, acting as such, is presumed to have acted in the lawful exercise of its jurisdiction. This presumption applies only when the act of the court or judge is under collateral attack.[1]

667. A person not heard from in five years is presumed to be dead.[29]

668. An unlawful intent is presumed from the doing of an unlawful act. This presumption is inapplicable in a criminal action to establish the specific intent of the defendant where specific intent is an element of the crime charged.[1]

669. (a) The failure of a person to exercise due care is presumed if:
(1) He violated a statute, ordinance, or regulation of a public entity;
(2) The violation proximately caused death or injury to person or property;
(3) The death or injury resulted from an occurrence of the nature which the statute, ordinance, or regulation was designed to prevent; and
(4) The person suffering the death or the injury to his person or property was one of the class of persons for whose protection the statute, ordinance, or regulation was adopted.
(b) This presumption may be rebutted by proof that:
(1) The person violating the statute, ordinance, or regulation did what might reasonably be expected of a person of ordinary prudence, acting under similar circumstances, who desired to comply with the law; or
(2) The person violating the statute, ordinance, or regulation was a child and exercised the degree of care ordinarily exercised by persons of his maturity, intelligence, and capacity under similar circumstances, but the presumption may not be rebutted by

such proof if the violation occurred in the course of an activity normally engaged in only by adults and requiring adult qualifications.[3]

669.1. A rule, policy, manual, or guideline of state or local government setting forth standards of conduct or guidelines for its employees in the conduct of their public employment shall not be considered a statute, ordinance, or regulation of that public entity within the meaning of Section 669, unless the rule, manual, policy, or guideline has been formally adopted as a statute, as an ordinance of a local governmental entity in this state empowered to adopt ordinances, or as a regulation by an agency of the state pursuant to the Administrative Procedure Act (Chapter 3.5 (commencing with Section 11340) of Division 3 of Title 2 of the Government Code), or by an agency of the United States government pursuant to the federal Administrative Procedure Act (Chapter 5 (commencing with Section 5001) of Title 5 of the United States Code). This section affects only the presumption set forth in Section 669, and is not otherwise intended to affect the admissibility or inadmissibility of the rule, policy, manual, or guideline under other provisions of law.[41]

669.5. (a) Any ordinance enacted by the governing body of a city, county, or city and county which (1) directly limits, by number, the building permits that may be issued for residential construction or the buildable lots which may be developed for residential purposes, or (2) changes the standards of residential development on vacant land so that the governing body's zoning is rendered in violation of Section 65913.1 of the Government Code is presumed to have an impact on the supply of residential units available in an area which includes territory outside the jurisdiction of the city, county, or city and county.

(b) With respect to any action which challenges the validity of an ordinance specified in subdivision (a) the city, county, or city and county enacting the ordinance shall bear the burden of proof that the ordinance is necessary for the protection of the public health, safety, or welfare of the population of the city, county, or city and county.

(c) This section does not apply to state and federal building code requirements or local ordinances which (1) impose a moratorium, to protect the public health and safety, on residential construction for a specified period of time, if, under the terms of the ordinance, the moratorium will cease when the public health or safety is no longer jeopardized by the construction, (2) create agricultural preserves under Chapter 7 (commencing with Section 51200) of Part 1 of Division 1 of Title 5 of the Government Code, or (3) restrict the number of buildable parcels or designate lands within a zone for nonresidential uses in order to protect agricultural uses as defined in subdivision (b) of Section 51201 of the Government Code or open-space land as defined in subdivision (h) of Section 65560 of the Government Code.

(d) This section shall not apply to a voter approved ordinance adopted by referendum or initiative prior to the effective date of this section which (1) requires the city, county, or city and county to establish a population growth limit which represents its fair share of each year's statewide population growth, or (2) which sets a growth rate of no more than the average population growth rate experienced by the state as a whole. Paragraph (2) of subdivision (a) does not apply to a voter-approved ordinance adopted by referendum or initiative which exempts housing affordable to persons and families of low or moderate income, as defined in Section 50093 of the Health and Safety Code, or which otherwise provides low- and moderate-income housing sites equivalent to such an exemption.[137]

670. (a) In any dispute concerning payment by means of a check, a copy of the check produced in accordance with Section 1550 of the Evidence Code, together with the original bank statement that reflects payment of the check by the bank on which it was drawn or a copy thereof produced in the same manner, creates a presumption that the check has been paid.
(b) As used in this section:
(1) "Bank" means any person engaged in the business of banking and includes, in addition to a commercial bank, a savings and loan association, savings bank, or credit union.
(2) "Check" means a draft, other than a documentary draft, payable on demand and drawn on a bank, even though it is described by another term, such as "share draft" or "negotiable order of withdrawal."[76]

DIVISION 6: WITNESSES

DIVISION 6 ENACTED BY STATS. 1965, CH. 299.
SECTION 700 - 795

Chapter 1: Competency

Chapter 1 enacted by Stats. 1965, Ch. 299.

700. Except as otherwise provided by statute, every person, irrespective of age, is qualified to be a witness and no person is disqualified to testify to any matter.[32]

701. (a) A person is disqualified to be a witness if he or she is:

(1) Incapable of expressing himself or herself concerning the matter so as to be understood, either directly or through interpretation by one who can understand him; or

(2) Incapable of understanding the duty of a witness to tell the truth.

(b) In any proceeding held outside the presence of a jury, the court may reserve challenges to the competency of a witness until the conclusion of the direct examination of that witness.[33]

702. (a) Subject to Section 801, the testimony of a witness concerning a particular matter is inadmissible unless he has personal knowledge of the matter. Against the objection of a party, such personal knowledge must be shown before the witness may testify concerning the matter.

(b) A witness' personal knowledge of a matter may be shown by any otherwise admissible evidence, including his own testimony.[1]

703. (a) Before the judge presiding at the trial of an action may be called to testify in that trial as a witness, he shall, in proceedings held out of the presence and hearing of the jury, inform the parties of the information he has concerning any fact or matter about which he will be called to testify.

(b) Against the objection of a party, the judge presiding at the trial of an action may not testify in that trial as a witness. Upon such objection, the judge shall declare a mistrial and order the action assigned for trial before another judge.

(c) The calling of the judge presiding at a trial to testify in that trial as a witness shall be deemed a consent to the granting of a motion for mistrial, and an objection to such calling of a judge shall be deemed a motion for mistrial.

(d) In the absence of objection by a party, the judge presiding at the trial of an action may testify in that trial as a witness.[1]

703.5. No person presiding at any judicial or quasi-judicial proceeding, and no arbitrator or mediator, shall be competent to testify, in any subsequent civil proceeding, as to any statement, conduct, decision, or ruling, occurring at or in conjunction with the prior proceeding, except as to a statement or conduct that could (a) give rise to civil or criminal contempt, (b) constitute a crime, (c) be the subject of investigation by the State Bar or Commission on Judicial Performance, or (d) give rise to disqualification proceedings under paragraph (1) or (6) of subdivision (a) of Section 170.1 of the Code of Civil Procedure. However, this section does not apply to a mediator with regard to any mediation under Chapter 11 (commencing with Section 3160) of

Part 2 of Division 8 of the Family Code.[57]

704. (a) Before a juror sworn and impaneled in the trial of an action may be called to testify before the jury in that trial as a witness, he shall, in proceedings conducted by the court out of the presence and hearing of the remaining jurors, inform the parties of the information he has concerning any fact or matter about which he will be called to testify.
(b) Against the objection of a party, a juror sworn and impaneled in the trial of an action may not testify before the jury in that trial as a witness. Upon such objection, the court shall declare a mistrial and order the action assigned for trial before another jury.
(c) The calling of a juror to testify before the jury as a witness shall be deemed a consent to the granting of a motion for mistrial, and an objection to such calling of a juror shall be deemed a motion for mistrial.
(d) In the absence of objection by a party, a juror sworn and impaneled in the trial of an action may be compelled to testify in that trial as a witness.[1]

Chapter 2: Oath and Confrontation

Chapter 2 enacted by Stats. 1965, Ch. 299.

710. Every witness before testifying shall take an oath or make an affirmation or declaration in the form provided by law, except that a child under the age of 10 or a dependent person with a substantial cognitive impairment, in the court's discretion, may be required only to promise to tell the truth.[95]

711. At the trial of an action, a witness can be heard only in the presence and subject to the examination of all the parties to the action, if they choose to attend and examine.[1]

712. Notwithstanding Sections 711 and 1200, at the trial of a criminal action, evidence of the technique used in taking blood samples may be given by a registered nurse, licensed vocational nurse, or licensed clinical laboratory technologist or clinical laboratory bioanalyst, by means of an affidavit. The affidavit shall be admissible, provided the party offering the affidavit as evidence has served all other parties to the action, or their counsel, with a copy of the affidavit no less than 10 days prior to trial. Nothing in this section shall preclude any party or his counsel from objecting to the introduction of the affidavit at any time, and requiring the attendance of the affiant, or compelling attendance by subpoena.[18]

Chapter 3: Expert Witnesses

Chapter 3 enacted by Stats. 1965, Ch. 299.

Article 1: Expert Witnesses Generally

Article 1 enacted by Stats. 1965, Ch. 299.

720. (a) A person is qualified to testify as an expert if he has special knowledge, skill, experience, training, or education sufficient to qualify him as an expert on the subject to which his testimony relates. Against the objection of a party, such special knowledge, skill, experience, training, or education must be shown before the witness may testify as an expert.
(b) A witness' special knowledge, skill, experience, training, or education may be shown by any otherwise admissible

evidence, including his own testimony.[1]

721. (a) Subject to subdivision (b), a witness testifying as an expert may be cross-examined to the same extent as any other witness and, in addition, may be fully cross-examined as to (1) his or her qualifications, (2) the subject to which his or her expert testimony relates, and (3) the matter upon which his or her opinion is based and the reasons for his or her opinion.
(b) If a witness testifying as an expert testifies in the form of an opinion, he or she may not be cross-examined in regard to the content or tenor of any scientific, technical, or professional text, treatise, journal, or similar publication unless any of the following occurs:
(1) The witness referred to, considered, or relied upon such publication in arriving at or forming his or her opinion.
(2) The publication has been admitted in evidence.
(3) The publication has been established as a reliable authority by the testimony or admission of the witness or by other expert testimony or by judicial notice.
If admitted, relevant portions of the publication may be read into evidence but may not be received as exhibits.[69]

722. (a) The fact of the appointment of an expert witness by the court may be revealed to the trier of fact.
(b) The compensation and expenses paid or to be paid to an expert witness by the party calling him is a proper subject of inquiry by any adverse party as relevant to the credibility of the witness and the weight of his testimony.[1]

723. The court may, at any time before or during the trial of an action, limit the number of expert witnesses to be called by any party.[1]

Article 2: Appointment of Expert Witness by Court
Article 2 enacted by Stats. 1965, Ch. 299.

730. When it appears to the court, at any time before or during the trial of an action, that expert evidence is or may be required by the court or by any party to the action, the court on its own motion or on motion of any party may appoint one or more experts to investigate, to render a report as may be ordered by the court, and to testify as an expert at the trial of the action relative to the fact or matter as to which the expert evidence is or may be required. The court may fix the compensation for these services, if any, rendered by any person appointed under this section, in addition to any service as a witness, at the amount as seems reasonable to the court.
Nothing in this section shall be construed to permit a person to perform any act for which a license is required unless the person holds the appropriate license to lawfully perform that act.[46]

731. (a) (1) In all criminal actions and juvenile court proceedings, the compensation fixed under Section 730 shall be a charge against the county in which the action or proceeding is pending and shall be paid out of the treasury of that county on order of the court.
(2) Notwithstanding paragraph (1), if the expert is appointed for the court's needs, the compensation shall be a charge against the court.

(b) In any county in which the superior court so provides, the compensation fixed under Section 730 for medical experts appointed for the court's needs in civil actions shall be a charge against the court. In any county in which the board of supervisors so provides, the compensation fixed under Section 730 for medical experts appointed in civil actions, for purposes other than the court's needs, shall be a charge against and paid out of the treasury of that county on order of the court.
(c) Except as otherwise provided in this section, in all civil actions, the compensation fixed under Section 730 shall, in the first instance, be apportioned and charged to the several parties in a proportion as the court may determine and may thereafter be taxed and allowed in like manner as other costs.[113]

732. Any expert appointed by the court under Section 730 may be called and examined by the court or by any party to the action. When such witness is called and examined by the court, the parties have the same right as is expressed in Section 775 to cross-examine the witness and to object to the questions asked and the evidence adduced.[1]

733. Nothing contained in this article shall be deemed or construed to prevent any party to any action from producing other expert evidence on the same fact or matter mentioned in Section 730; but, where other expert witnesses are called by a party to the action, their fees shall be paid by the party calling them and only ordinary witness fees shall be taxed as costs in the action.[1]

Chapter 4: Interpreters and Translators

Chapter 4 enacted by Stats. 1965, Ch. 299.

750. A person who serves as an interpreter or translator in any action is subject to all the rules of law relating to witnesses.[1]

751. (a) An interpreter shall take an oath that he or she will make a true interpretation to the witness in a language that the witness understands and that he or she will make a true interpretation of the witness' answers to questions to counsel, court, or jury, in the English language, with his or her best skill and judgment.
(b) In any proceeding in which a deaf or hard-of-hearing person is testifying under oath, the interpreter certified pursuant to subdivision (f) of Section 754 shall advise the court whenever he or she is unable to comply with his or her oath taken pursuant to subdivision (a).
(c) A translator shall take an oath that he or she will make a true translation in the English language of any writing he or she is to decipher or translate.
(d) An interpreter regularly employed by the court and certified or registered in accordance with Article 4 (commencing with Section 68560) of Chapter 2 of Title 8 of the Government Code, or a translator regularly employed by the court, may file an oath as prescribed by this section with the clerk of the court. The filed oath shall serve for all subsequent court proceedings until the appointment is revoked by the court.[65]

752. (a) When a witness is incapable of understanding the English language or is incapable of expressing himself or herself in the English language so as to

be understood directly by counsel, court, and jury, an interpreter whom the witness can understand and who can understand the witness shall be sworn to interpret for the witness.

(b) The record shall identify the interpreter, who may be appointed and compensated as provided in Article 2 (commencing with Section 730) of Chapter 3, with that compensation charged as follows:

(1) In all criminal actions and juvenile court proceedings, the compensation for an interpreter under this section shall be a charge against the court.

(2) In all civil actions, the compensation for an interpreter under this section shall, in the first instance, be apportioned and charged to the several parties in a proportion as the court may determine and may thereafter be taxed and allowed in a like manner as other costs.[114]

753. (a) When the written characters in a writing offered in evidence are incapable of being deciphered or understood directly, a translator who can decipher the characters or understand the language shall be sworn to decipher or translate the writing.

(b) The record shall identify the translator, who may be appointed and compensated as provided in Article 2 (commencing with Section 730) of Chapter 3, with that compensation charged as follows:

(1) In all criminal actions and juvenile court proceedings, the compensation for a translator under this section shall be a charge against the court.

(2) In all civil actions, the compensation for a translator under this section shall, in the first instance, be apportioned and charged to the several parties in a proportion as the court may determine and may thereafter be taxed and allowed in like manner as other costs.[115]

754. (a) As used in this section, "individual who is deaf or hard of hearing" means an individual with a hearing loss so great as to prevent his or her understanding language spoken in a normal tone, but does not include an individual who is hard of hearing provided with, and able to fully participate in the proceedings through the use of, an assistive listening system or computer-aided transcription equipment provided pursuant to Section 54.8 of the Civil Code.

(b) In a civil or criminal action, including an action involving a traffic or other infraction, a small claims court proceeding, a juvenile court proceeding, a family court proceeding or service, or a proceeding to determine the mental competency of a person, in a court-ordered or court-provided alternative dispute resolution, including mediation and arbitration, or in an administrative hearing, where a party or witness is an individual who is deaf or hard of hearing and the individual who is deaf or hard of hearing is present and participating, the proceeding shall be interpreted in a language that the individual who is deaf or hard of hearing understands by a qualified interpreter appointed by the court or other appointing authority, or as agreed upon.

(c) For purposes of this section, "appointing authority" means a court, department, board, commission, agency, licensing or legislative body, or other body for proceedings requiring a qualified interpreter.

(d) For purposes of this section, "interpreter" includes an oral interpreter, a sign language interpreter, or a deaf-blind interpreter, depending upon the needs of the individual who is deaf or hard of hearing.

(e) For purposes of this section, "intermediary interpreter" means an individual who is deaf or hard of hearing, or a hearing individual who is able to assist in providing an accurate interpretation between spoken English and sign language or between variants of sign language or between American Sign Language and other foreign languages by acting as an intermediary between the individual who is deaf or hard of hearing and the qualified interpreter.

(f) For purposes of this section, "qualified interpreter" means an interpreter who has been certified as competent to interpret court proceedings by a testing organization, agency, or educational institution approved by the Judicial Council as qualified to administer tests to court interpreters for individuals who are deaf or hard of hearing.

(g) If the appointed interpreter is not familiar with the use of particular signs by the individual who is deaf or hard of hearing or his or her particular variant of sign language, the court or other appointing authority shall, in consultation with the individual who is deaf or hard of hearing or his or her representative, appoint an intermediary interpreter.

(h) (1) Before July 1, 1992, the Judicial Council shall conduct a study to establish the guidelines pursuant to which it shall determine which testing organizations, agencies, or educational institutions will be approved to administer tests for certification of court interpreters for individuals who are deaf or hard of hearing. It is the intent of the Legislature that the study obtain the widest possible input from the public, including, but not limited to, educational institutions, the judiciary, linguists, members of the State Bar of California, court interpreters, members of professional interpreting organizations, and members of the deaf and hard of hearing communities. After obtaining public comment and completing its study, the Judicial Council shall publish these guidelines. By January 1, 1997, the Judicial Council shall approve one or more entities to administer testing for court interpreters for individuals who are deaf or hard of hearing. Testing entities may include educational institutions, testing organizations, joint powers agencies, or public agencies.

(2) Commencing July 1, 1997, court interpreters for individuals who are deaf or hard of hearing shall meet the qualifications specified in subdivision (f).

(i) Persons appointed to serve as interpreters under this section shall be paid, in addition to actual travel costs, the prevailing rate paid to persons employed by the court to provide other interpreter services unless such service is considered to be a part of the person's regular duties as an employee of the state, county, or other political subdivision of the state. Except as provided in subdivision (j), payment of the interpreter's fee shall be a charge against the court. Payment of the interpreter's fee in administrative proceedings shall be a charge against the appointing board or authority.

(j) Whenever a peace officer or any other person having a law enforcement or prosecutorial function in a criminal or quasi-criminal investigation or non-court proceeding questions or otherwise interviews an alleged victim or witness who demonstrates or alleges deafness or hearing loss, a good faith effort to secure the services of an interpreter shall be made without any unnecessary delay, unless either the individual who is deaf or hard of hearing affirmatively indicates that he or she does not need or cannot use an interpreter, or an interpreter is not otherwise required by Title II of the federal Americans with Disabilities Act of 1990 (Public Law 101-336) and federal regulations adopted thereunder. Payment of the interpreter's fee shall be a charge against the county, or other political subdivision of the state, in which the action is pending.

(k) A statement, written or oral, made by an individual who the court finds is deaf or hard of hearing in reply to a question of a peace officer, or any other person having a law enforcement or prosecutorial function in a criminal or quasi-criminal investigation or proceeding, shall not be used against that individual who is deaf or hard of hearing unless the question was accurately interpreted and the statement was made knowingly, voluntarily, and intelligently and was accurately interpreted, or the court finds that either the individual could not have used an interpreter or an interpreter was not otherwise required by Title II of the federal Americans with Disabilities Act of 1990 (Public Law 101-336) and federal regulations adopted thereunder and that the statement was made knowingly, voluntarily, and intelligently.

(l) In obtaining services of an interpreter for purposes of subdivision (j) or (k), priority shall be given to first obtaining a qualified interpreter.

(m) Subdivisions (j) and (k) shall not be deemed to supersede the requirement of subdivision (b) for use of a qualified interpreter for an individual who is deaf or hard of hearing participating as a party or witness in a trial or hearing.

(n) In an action or proceeding in which an individual who is deaf or hard of hearing is a participant, the appointing authority shall not commence the action or proceeding until the appointed interpreter is in full view of and spatially situated to assure proper communication with the participating individual who is deaf or hard of hearing.

(o) Each superior court shall maintain a current roster of qualified interpreters certified pursuant to subdivision (f).[140]

754.5. Whenever an otherwise valid privilege exists between an individual who is deaf or hard of hearing and another person, that privilege is not waived merely because an interpreter was used to facilitate their communication.[132]

755.5. (a) During any medical examination, requested by an insurer or by the defendant, of a person who is a party to a civil action and who does not proficiently speak or understand the English language, conducted for the purpose of determining damages in a civil action, an interpreter shall be present to interpret the examination in a language that the person understands. The interpreter shall be certified pursuant to Article 8 (commencing with Section 11435.05) of Chapter 4.5 of Part 1 of Division 3 of Title 2 of the Government Code.

(b) The fees of interpreters used under subdivision (a) shall be paid by the insurer or defendant requesting the medical examination.

(c) The record of, or testimony concerning, any medical examination conducted in violation of subdivision (a) shall be inadmissible in the civil action for which it was conducted or any other civil action.

(d) This section does not prohibit the presence of any other person to assist a party.

(e) In the event that interpreters certified pursuant to Article 8 (commencing with Section 11435.05) of Chapter 4.5 of Part 1 of Division 3 of Title 2 of the Government Code cannot be present at the medical examination, upon stipulation of the parties the requester specified in subdivision (a) shall have the discretionary authority to provisionally qualify and use other interpreters.[61]

756. (a) To the extent required by other state or federal laws, the Judicial Council shall reimburse courts for court interpreter services provided in civil actions and proceedings to any party who is present in court and who does not proficiently speak or understand the English language for the purpose of interpreting the proceedings in a language the party understands, and assisting communications between the party, the party's attorney, and the court.

(b) If sufficient funds are not appropriated to provide an interpreter to every party that meets the standard of eligibility, court interpreter services in civil cases reimbursed by the Judicial Council, pursuant to subdivision (a), shall be prioritized by case type by each court in the following order:

(1) Actions and proceedings under Division 10 (commencing with Section 6200) of the Family Code, actions or proceedings under the Uniform Parentage Act (Part 3 (commencing with Section 7600) of Division 12 of the Family Code) in which a protective order has been granted or is being sought pursuant to Section 6221 of the Family Code, and actions and proceedings for dissolution or nullity of marriage or legal separation of the parties in which a protective order has been granted or is being sought pursuant to Section 6221 of the Family Code; actions and proceedings under subdivision (y) of Section 527.6 of the Code of Civil Procedure; and actions and proceedings for physical abuse or neglect under the Elder Abuse and Dependent Adult Civil Protection Act (Chapter 11 (commencing with Section 15600) of Part 3 of Division 9 of the Welfare and Institutions Code).

(2) Actions and proceedings relating to unlawful detainer.

(3) Actions and proceedings to terminate parental rights.

(4) Actions and proceedings relating to conservatorship or guardianship, including the appointment or termination of a probate guardian or conservator.

(5) Actions and proceedings by a parent to obtain sole legal or physical custody of a child or rights to visitation.

(6) All other actions and proceedings under Section 527.6 of the Code of Civil Procedure or the Elder Abuse and Dependent Adult Civil Protection Act (Chapter 11 (commencing with Section 15600) of Part 3 of Division 9 of the Welfare and Institutions Code).

(7) All other actions and proceedings related to family law.

(8) All other civil actions or proceedings.

(c) (1) If funds are not available to provide an interpreter to every party that meets the standard of eligibility, preference shall be given for parties proceeding in forma pauperis pursuant to Section 68631 of the Government Code in any civil action or proceeding described in paragraph (3), (4), (5), (6), (7), or (8) of subdivision (b).

(2) Courts may provide an interpreter to a party outside the priority order listed in subdivision (b) when a qualified interpreter is present and available at the court location and no higher priority action that meets the standard of eligibility described in subdivision (a) is taking place at that location during the period of time for which the interpreter has already been compensated.

(d) A party shall not be charged a fee for the provision of a court interpreter.

(e) In seeking reimbursement for court interpreter services, the court shall identify to the Judicial Council the case types for which the interpretation to be reimbursed was provided. Courts shall regularly certify that in providing the interpreter services, they have complied with the priorities and preferences set forth in subdivisions (b) and (c), which shall be subject to review by the Judicial Council.

(f) This section shall not be construed to alter, limit, or negate any right to an interpreter in a civil action or proceeding otherwise provided by state or federal law, or the right to an interpreter in criminal, traffic, or other infraction, juvenile, or mental competency actions or proceedings.

(g) This section shall not result in a reduction in staffing or compromise the quality of interpreting services in criminal, juvenile, or other types of matters in which interpreters are provided.[154]

757. Pursuant to this chapter, other applicable law, and existing Judicial Council policy, including the policy adopted on January 23, 2014, existing authority to provide interpreters in civil court includes the authority to provide an interpreter in a proceeding in which a petitioner requests an order from the superior court to make the findings regarding special immigrant juvenile status pursuant to Section 1101(a)(27)(J) of Title 8 of the United States Code.[121]

Chapter 5: Method and Scope of Examination

Chapter 5 enacted by Stats. 1965, Ch. 299.

Article 1: Definitions

Article 1 enacted by Stats. 1965, Ch. 299.

760. “Direct examination” is the first examination of a witness upon a matter that is not within the scope of a previous examination of the witness.[1]

761. “Cross-examination” is the examination of a witness by a party other than the direct examiner upon a matter that is within the scope of the direct examination of the witness.[1]

762. “Redirect examination” is an examination of a witness by the direct examiner subsequent to the cross-examination of the witness.[1]

763. “Recross-examination” is an examination of a witness by a cross-examiner subsequent to a redirect examination of the witness.[1]

764. A “leading question” is a question that suggests to the witness the answer

that the examining party desires.[1]

Article 2: Examination of Witnesses
Article 2 enacted by Stats. 1965, Ch. 299.

765. (a) The court shall exercise reasonable control over the mode of interrogation of a witness so as to make interrogation as rapid, as distinct, and as effective for the ascertainment of the truth, as may be, and to protect the witness from undue harassment or embarrassment.
(b) With a witness under the age of 14 or a dependent person with a substantial cognitive impairment, the court shall take special care to protect him or her from undue harassment or embarrassment, and to restrict the unnecessary repetition of questions. The court shall also take special care to ensure that questions are stated in a form which is appropriate to the age or cognitive level of the witness. The court may, in the interests of justice, on objection by a party, forbid the asking of a question which is in a form that is not reasonably likely to be understood by a person of the age or cognitive level of the witness.[96]

766. A witness must give responsive answers to questions, and answers that are not responsive shall be stricken on motion of any party.[1]

767. (a) Except under special circumstances where the interests of justice otherwise require:
(1) A leading question may not be asked of a witness on direct or redirect examination.
(2) A leading question may be asked of a witness on cross-examination or recross-examination.
(b) The court may, in the interests of justice permit a leading question to be asked of a child under 10 years of age or a dependent person with a substantial cognitive impairment in a case involving a prosecution under Section 273a, 273d, 288.5, 368, or any of the acts described in Section 11165.1 or 11165.2 of the Penal Code. [97]

768. (a) In examining a witness concerning a writing, it is not necessary to show, read, or disclose to him any part of the writing.
(b) If a writing is shown to a witness, all parties to the action must be given an opportunity to inspect it before any question concerning it may be asked of the witness.[1]

769. In examining a witness concerning a statement or other conduct by him that is inconsistent with any part of his testimony at the hearing, it is not necessary to disclose to him any information concerning the statement or other conduct.[1]

770. Unless the interests of justice otherwise require, extrinsic evidence of a statement made by a witness that is inconsistent with any part of his testimony at the hearing shall be excluded unless:
(a) The witness was so examined while testifying as to give him an opportunity to explain or to deny the statement; or
(b) The witness has not been excused from giving further testimony in the action.[1]

771. (a) Subject to subdivision (c), if a witness, either while testifying or prior thereto, uses a writing to refresh his memory with respect to any matter about which he testifies, such writing must be produced at the hearing at the request of an adverse party and, unless

the writing is so produced, the testimony of the witness concerning such matter shall be stricken.

(b) If the writing is produced at the hearing, the adverse party may, if he chooses, inspect the writing, cross-examine the witness concerning it, and introduce in evidence such portion of it as may be pertinent to the testimony of the witness.

(c) Production of the writing is excused, and the testimony of the witness shall not be stricken, if the writing:

(1) Is not in the possession or control of the witness or the party who produced his testimony concerning the matter; and

(2) Was not reasonably procurable by such party through the use of the court's process or other available means.[1]

772. (a) The examination of a witness shall proceed in the following phases: direct examination, cross-examination, redirect examination, recross-examination, and continuing thereafter by redirect and recross-examination.

(b) Unless for good cause the court otherwise directs, each phase of the examination of a witness must be concluded before the succeeding phase begins.

(c) Subject to subdivision (d), a party may, in the discretion of the court, interrupt his cross-examination, redirect examination, or recross-examination of a witness, in order to examine the witness upon a matter not within the scope of a previous examination of the witness.

(d) If the witness is the defendant in a criminal action, the witness may not, without his consent, be examined under direct examination by another party.[1]

773. (a) A witness examined by one party may be cross-examined upon any matter within the scope of the direct examination by each other party to the action in such order as the court directs.

(b) The cross-examination of a witness by any party whose interest is not adverse to the party calling him is subject to the same rules that are applicable to the direct examination.[1]

774. A witness once examined cannot be reexamined as to the same matter without leave of the court, but he may be reexamined as to any new matter upon which he has been examined by another party to the action. Leave may be granted or withheld in the court's discretion.[1]

775. The court, on its own motion or on the motion of any party, may call witnesses and interrogate them the same as if they had been produced by a party to the action, and the parties may object to the questions asked and the evidence adduced the same as if such witnesses were called and examined by an adverse party. Such witnesses may be cross-examined by all parties to the action in such order as the court directs.[1]

776. (a) A party to the record of any civil action, or a person identified with such a party, may be called and examined as if under cross-examination by any adverse party at any time during the presentation of evidence by the party calling the witness.

(b) A witness examined by a party under this section may be cross-examined by all other parties to the action in such order as the court directs; but, subject to subdivision (e), the witness may be examined only as if under redirect examination by:

(1) In the case of a witness who is a party, his own counsel and counsel for a party who is not adverse to the witness.

(2) In the case of a witness who is not a party, counsel for the party with whom the witness is identified and counsel for a party who is not adverse to the party with whom the witness is identified.

(c) For the purpose of this section, parties represented by the same counsel are deemed to be a single party.

(d) For the purpose of this section, a person is identified with a party if he is:

(1) A person for whose immediate benefit the action is prosecuted or defended by the party.

(2) A director, officer, superintendent, member, agent, employee, or managing agent of the party or of a person specified in paragraph (1), or any public employee of a public entity when such public entity is the party.

(3) A person who was in any of the relationships specified in paragraph (2) at the time of the act or omission giving rise to the cause of action.

(4) A person who was in any of the relationships specified in paragraph (2) at the time he obtained knowledge of the matter concerning which he is sought to be examined under this section.

(e) Paragraph (2) of subdivision (b) does not require counsel for the party with whom the witness is identified and counsel for a party who is not adverse to the party with whom the witness is identified to examine the witness as if under redirect examination if the party who called the witness for examination under this section:

(1) Is also a person identified with the same party with whom the witness is identified.

(2) Is the personal representative, heir, successor, or assignee of a person identified with the same party with whom the witness is identified.[4]

777. (a) Subject to subdivisions (b) and (c), the court may exclude from the courtroom any witness not at the time under examination so that such witness cannot hear the testimony of other witnesses.

(b) A party to the action cannot be excluded under this section.

(c) If a person other than a natural person is a party to the action, an officer or employee designated by its attorney is entitled to be present.[1]

778. After a witness has been excused from giving further testimony in the action, he cannot be recalled without leave of the court. Leave may be granted or withheld in the court's discretion.[1]

Chapter 6: Credibility of Witnesses

Chapter 6 enacted by Stats. 1965, Ch. 299.

Article 1: Credibility Generally

Article 1 enacted by Stats. 1965, Ch. 299.

780. Except as otherwise provided by statute, the court or jury may consider in determining the credibility of a witness any matter that has any tendency in reason to prove or disprove the truthfulness of his testimony at the

hearing, including but not limited to any of the following:

(a) His demeanor while testifying and the manner in which he testifies.

(b) The character of his testimony.

(c) The extent of his capacity to perceive, to recollect, or to communicate any matter about which he testifies.

(d) The extent of his opportunity to perceive any matter about which he testifies.

(e) His character for honesty or veracity or their opposites.

(f) The existence or nonexistence of a bias, interest, or other motive.

(g) A statement previously made by him that is consistent with his testimony at the hearing.

(h) A statement made by him that is inconsistent with any part of his testimony at the hearing.

(i) The existence or nonexistence of any fact testified to by him.

(j) His attitude toward the action in which he testifies or toward the giving of testimony.

(k) His admission of untruthfulness.[1]

782. (a) In any of the circumstances described in subdivision (c), if evidence of sexual conduct of the complaining witness is offered to attack the credibility of the complaining witness under Section 780, the following procedure shall be followed:

(1) A written motion shall be made by the defendant to the court and prosecutor stating that the defense has an offer of proof of the relevance of evidence of the sexual conduct of the complaining witness that is proposed to be presented and of its relevance in attacking the credibility of the complaining witness.

(2) The written motion shall be accompanied by an affidavit in which the offer of proof shall be stated. The affidavit shall be filed under seal and only unsealed by the court to determine if the offer of proof is sufficient to order a hearing pursuant to paragraph (3). After that determination, the affidavit shall be resealed by the court.

(3) If the court finds that the offer of proof is sufficient, the court shall order a hearing out of the presence of the jury, if any, and at the hearing allow the questioning of the complaining witness regarding the offer of proof made by the defendant.

(4) At the conclusion of the hearing, if the court finds that evidence proposed to be offered by the defendant regarding the sexual conduct of the complaining witness is relevant pursuant to Section 780, and is not inadmissible pursuant to Section 352, the court may make an order stating what evidence may be introduced by the defendant, and the nature of the questions to be permitted. The defendant may then offer evidence pursuant to the order of the court.

(5) An affidavit resealed by the court pursuant to paragraph (2) shall remain sealed, unless the defendant raises an issue on appeal or collateral review relating to the offer of proof contained in the sealed document. If the defendant raises that issue on appeal, the court shall allow the Attorney General and appellate counsel for the defendant access to the sealed affidavit. If the issue is raised on collateral review, the court shall allow the district attorney and defendant's counsel access to the sealed affidavit. The use of the information contained in the affidavit shall be limited solely to the pending proceeding.

(b) (1) As used in this section, "complaining witness" means:

(A) The alleged victim of the crime charged, the prosecution of which is subject to this section, pursuant to paragraph (1) of subdivision (c).

(B) An alleged victim offering testimony pursuant to paragraph (2) or (3) of subdivision (c).

(2) As used in this section, "evidence of sexual conduct" includes those portions of a social media account about the complaining witness, including any text, image, video, or picture, which depict sexual content, sexual history, nudity or partial nudity, intimate sexual activity, communications about sex, sexual fantasies, and other information that appeals to a prurient interest, unless it is related to the alleged offense.

(c) The procedure provided by subdivision (a) shall apply in any of the following circumstances:

(1) In a prosecution under Section 261, 262, 264.1, 286, 287, 288, 288.5, or 289 of, or former Section 288a of, the Penal Code, or for assault with intent to commit, attempt to commit, or conspiracy to commit any crime defined in any of those sections, except if the crime is alleged to have occurred in a local detention facility, as defined in Section 6031.4 of the Penal Code, or in the state prison, as defined in Section 4504.

(2) When an alleged victim testifies pursuant to subdivision (b) of Section 1101 as a victim of a crime listed in Section 243.4, 261, 261.5, 269, 285, 286, 287, 288, 288.5, 289, 314, or 647.6 of, or former Section 288a of, the Penal Code, except if the crime is alleged to have occurred in a local detention facility, as defined in Section 6031.4 of the Penal Code, or in the state prison, as defined in Section 4504 of the Penal Code.

(3) When an alleged victim of a sexual offense testifies pursuant to Section 1108, except if the crime is alleged to have occurred in a local detention facility, as defined in Section 6031.4 of the possession of a condom is not admissible as evidence in the prosecution of a violation of Section 372 of, or subdivision Penal Code, or in the state prison, as defined in Section 4504 of the Penal Code.[159]

782.1. The (a) or (b) of Section 647 of, or former Section 653.22 of, the Penal Code, if the offense is related to prostitution.[166]

783. In any civil action alleging conduct which constitutes sexual harassment, sexual assault, or sexual battery, if evidence of sexual conduct of the plaintiff is offered to attack credibility of the plaintiff under Section 780, the following procedures shall be followed:

(a) A written motion shall be made by the defendant to the court and the plaintiff's attorney stating that the defense has an offer of proof of the relevancy of evidence of the sexual conduct of the plaintiff proposed to be presented.

(b) The written motion shall be accompanied by an affidavit in which the offer of proof shall be stated.

(c) If the court finds that the offer of proof is sufficient, the court shall order a hearing out of the presence of the jury, if any, and at the hearing allow the questioning of the plaintiff regarding the offer of proof made by the defendant.

(d) At the conclusion of the hearing, if the court finds that evidence proposed to be offered by the defendant regarding the sexual conduct of the plaintiff is relevant pursuant to Section 780, and is not inadmissible pursuant to Section 352, the court may make an order stating what evidence may be introduced by the defendant, and the nature of the questions to be permitted. The defendant may then offer evidence pursuant to the order of the court.[34]

Article 2: Attacking or Supporting Credibility

Article 2 enacted by Stats. 1965, Ch. 299.

785. The credibility of a witness may be attacked or supported by any party, including the party calling him.[1]

786. Evidence of traits of his character other than honesty or veracity, or their opposites, is inadmissible to attack or support the credibility of a witness.[1]

787. Subject to Section 788, evidence of specific instances of his conduct relevant only as tending to prove a trait of his character is inadmissible to attack or support the credibility of a witness.[1]

788. For the purpose of attacking the credibility of a witness, it may be shown by the examination of the witness or by the record of the judgment that he has been convicted of a felony unless:

(a) A pardon based on his innocence has been granted to the witness by the jurisdiction in which he was convicted.

(b) A certificate of rehabilitation and pardon has been granted to the witness under the provisions of Chapter 3.5 (commencing with Section 4852.01) of Title 6 of Part 3 of the Penal Code.

(c) The accusatory pleading against the witness has been dismissed under the provisions of Penal Code Section 1203.4, but this exception does not apply to any criminal trial where the witness is being prosecuted for a subsequent offense.

(d) The conviction was under the laws of another jurisdiction and the witness has been relieved of the penalties and disabilities arising from the conviction pursuant to a procedure substantially equivalent to that referred to in subdivision (b) or (c).[1]

789. Evidence of his religious belief or lack thereof is inadmissible to attack or support the credibility of a witness.[1]

790. Evidence of the good character of a witness is inadmissible to support his credibility unless evidence of his bad character has been admitted for the purpose of attacking his credibility.[1]

791. Evidence of a statement previously made by a witness that is consistent with his testimony at the hearing is inadmissible to support his credibility unless it is offered after:

(a) Evidence of a statement made by him that is inconsistent with any part of his testimony at the hearing has been admitted for the purpose of attacking his credibility, and the statement was made before the alleged inconsistent statement; or

(b) An express or implied charge has been made that his testimony at the hearing is recently fabricated or is influenced by bias or other improper motive, and the statement was made before the bias, motive for fabrication, or other improper motive is alleged to have arisen.[1]

Chapter 7: Hypnosis of Witnesses

Chapter 7 added by Stats. 1984, Ch. 479, Sec. 1.

795. (a) The testimony of a witness is not inadmissible in a criminal proceeding by reason of the fact that the witness has previously undergone hypnosis for the purpose of recalling events that are the subject of the witness's testimony, if all of the following conditions are met:

(1) The testimony is limited to those matters that the witness recalled and related prior to the hypnosis.

(2) The substance of the prehypnotic memory was preserved in a writing, audio recording, or video recording prior to the hypnosis.

(3) The hypnosis was conducted in accordance with all of the following procedures:

(A) A written record was made prior to hypnosis documenting the subject's description of the event, and information that was provided to the hypnotist concerning the subject matter of the hypnosis.

(B) The subject gave informed consent to the hypnosis.

(C) The hypnosis session, including the pre- and post-hypnosis interviews, was video recorded for subsequent review.

(D) The hypnosis was performed by a licensed physician and surgeon, psychologist, licensed clinical social worker, licensed marriage and family therapist, or licensed professional clinical counselor experienced in the use of hypnosis and independent of and not in the presence of law enforcement, the prosecution, or the defense.

(4) Prior to admission of the testimony, the court holds a hearing pursuant to Section 402 at which the proponent of the evidence proves by clear and convincing evidence that the hypnosis did not so affect the witness as to render the witness's prehypnosis recollection unreliable or to substantially impair the ability to cross-examine the witness concerning the witness's prehypnosis recollection. At the hearing, each side shall have the right to present expert testimony and to cross-examine witnesses.

(b) Nothing in this section shall be construed to limit the ability of a party to attack the credibility of a witness who has undergone hypnosis, or to limit other legal grounds to admit or exclude the testimony of that witness.[111]

DIVISION 7: OPINION TESTIMONY AND SCIENTIFIC EVIDENCE

DIVISION 7 ENACTED BY STATS. 1965, CH. 299.
SECTION 800 - 870

Chapter 1: Expert and Other Opinion Testimony

Chapter 1 enacted by Stats. 1965, Ch. 299.

Article 1: Expert and Other Opinion Testimony Generally
Article 1 enacted by Stats. 1965, Ch. 299.

800. If a witness is not testifying as an expert, his testimony in the form of an opinion is limited to such an opinion as is permitted by law, including but not limited to an opinion that is:
(a) Rationally based on the perception of the witness; and
(b) Helpful to a clear understanding of his testimony.[1]

801. If a witness is testifying as an expert, his testimony in the form of an opinion is limited to such an opinion as is:
(a) Related to a subject that is sufficiently beyond common experience that the opinion of an expert would assist the trier of fact; and
(b) Based on matter (including his special knowledge, skill, experience, training, and education) perceived by or personally known to the witness or made known to him at or before the hearing, whether or not admissible, that is of a type that reasonably may be relied upon by an expert in forming an opinion upon the subject to which his testimony relates, unless an expert is precluded by law from using such matter as a basis for his opinion.[1]

801.1. (a) In a general civil case, as defined in Rule 1.6 of the California Rules of Court, where the party bearing the burden of proof proffers expert testimony regarding medical causation and where that party's expert is required as a condition of testifying to opine that causation exists to a reasonable medical probability, the party not bearing the burden of proof may offer a contrary expert only if its expert is able to opine that the proffered alternative cause or causes each exists to a reasonable medical probability, except as provided in subdivision (b).
(b) Subdivision (a) does not preclude a witness testifying as an expert from testifying that a matter cannot meet a reasonable degree of probability in the applicable field, and providing the basis for that opinion.[171]

802. A witness testifying in the form of an opinion may state on direct examination the reasons for his opinion and the matter (including, in the case of an expert, his special knowledge, skill, experience, training, and education) upon which it is based, unless he is precluded by law from using such reasons or matter as a basis for his opinion. The court in its discretion may require that a witness before testifying in the form of an opinion be first examined concerning the matter upon which his opinion is based.[1]

803. The court may, and upon objection shall, exclude testimony in the

form of an opinion that is based in whole or in significant part on matter that is not a proper basis for such an opinion. In such case, the witness may, if there remains a proper basis for his opinion, then state his opinion after excluding from consideration the matter determined to be improper.[1]

804. (a) If a witness testifying as an expert testifies that his opinion is based in whole or in part upon the opinion or statement of another person, such other person may be called and examined by any adverse party as if under cross-examination concerning the opinion or statement.
(b) This section is not applicable if the person upon whose opinion or statement the expert witness has relied is (1) a party, (2) a person identified with a party within the meaning of subdivision (d) of Section 776, or (3) a witness who has testified in the action concerning the subject matter of the opinion or statement upon which the expert witness has relied.
(c) Nothing in this section makes admissible an expert opinion that is inadmissible because it is based in whole or in part on the opinion or statement of another person.
(d) An expert opinion otherwise admissible is not made inadmissible by this section because it is based on the opinion or statement of a person who is unavailable for examination pursuant to this section.[1]

805. Testimony in the form of an opinion that is otherwise admissible is not objectionable because it embraces the ultimate issue to be decided by the trier of fact.[1]

Article 2: Evidence of Market Value of Property
Heading of Article 2 amended by Stats. 1978, Ch. 294.

810. (a) Except where another rule is provided by statute, this article provides special rules of evidence applicable to any action in which the value of property is to be ascertained.
(b) This article does not govern ad valorem property tax assessment or equalization proceedings.[22]

811. As used in this article, "value of property" means market value of any of the following:
(a) Real property or any interest therein.
(b) Real property or any interest therein and tangible personal property valued as a unit.[22]

812. This article is not intended to alter or change the existing substantive law, whether statutory or decisional, interpreting the meaning of "market value," whether denominated "fair market value" or otherwise.[19]

813. (a) The value of property may be shown only by the opinions of any of the following:
(1) Witnesses qualified to express such opinions.
(2) The owner or the spouse of the owner of the property or property interest being valued.
(3) An officer, regular employee, or partner designated by a corporation, partnership, or unincorporated association that is the owner of the property or property interest being valued, if the designee is knowledgeable as to the value of the property or property interest.

(b) Nothing in this section prohibits a view of the property being valued or the admission of any other admissible evidence (including but not limited to evidence as to the nature and condition of the property and, in an eminent domain proceeding, the character of the improvement proposed to be constructed by the plaintiff) for the limited purpose of enabling the court, jury, or referee to understand and weigh the testimony given under subdivision (a); and such evidence, except evidence of the character of the improvement proposed to be constructed by the plaintiff in an eminent domain proceeding, is subject to impeachment and rebuttal.

(c) For the purposes of subdivision (a), "owner of the property or property interest being valued" includes, but is not limited to, the following persons:

(1) A person entitled to possession of the property.

(2) Either party in an action or proceeding to determine the ownership of the property between the parties if the court determines that it would not be in the interest of efficient administration of justice to determine the issue of ownership prior to the admission of the opinion of the party.[22]

814. The opinion of a witness as to the value of property is limited to such an opinion as is based on matter perceived by or personally known to the witness or made known to the witness at or before the hearing, whether or not admissible, that is of a type that reasonably may be relied upon by an expert in forming an opinion as to the value of property, including but not limited to the matters listed in Sections 815 to 821, inclusive, unless a witness is precluded by law from using such matter as a basis for an opinion.[22]

815. When relevant to the determination of the value of property, a witness may take into account as a basis for an opinion the price and other terms and circumstances of any sale or contract to sell and purchase which included the property or property interest being valued or any part thereof if the sale or contract was freely made in good faith within a reasonable time before or after the date of valuation, except that in an eminent domain proceeding where the sale or contract to sell and purchase includes only the property or property interest being taken or a part thereof, such sale or contract to sell and purchase may not be taken into account if it occurs after the filing of the lis pendens.[19]

816. When relevant to the determination of the value of property, a witness may take into account as a basis for his opinion the price and other terms and circumstances of any sale or contract to sell and purchase comparable property if the sale or contract was freely made in good faith within a reasonable time before or after the date of valuation. In order to be considered comparable, the sale or contract must have been made sufficiently near in time to the date of valuation, and the property sold must be located sufficiently near the property being valued, and must be sufficiently alike in respect to character, size, situation, usability, and improvements, to make it clear that the property sold and the property being valued are comparable in value and that the price realized for the property sold may fairly be considered as shedding light on the value of the property being valued.[2]

817. (a) Subject to subdivision (b), when relevant to the determination of the value of property, a witness may take into account as a basis for an opinion the rent reserved and other terms and circumstances of any lease which included the property or property interest being valued or any part thereof which was in effect within a reasonable time before or after the date of valuation, except that in an eminent domain proceeding where the lease includes only the property or property interest being taken or a part thereof, such lease may not be taken into account in the determination of the value of property if it is entered into after the filing of the lis pendens.
(b) A witness may take into account a lease providing for a rental fixed by a percentage or other measurable portion of gross sales or gross income from a business conducted on the leased property only for the purpose of arriving at an opinion as to the reasonable net rental value attributable to the property or property interest being valued as provided in Section 819 or determining the value of a leasehold interest.[19]

818. For the purpose of determining the capitalized value of the reasonable net rental value attributable to the property or property interest being valued as provided in Section 819 or determining the value of a leasehold interest, a witness may take into account as a basis for his opinion the rent reserved and other terms and circumstances of any lease of comparable property if the lease was freely made in good faith within a reasonable time before or after the date of valuation.[2]

819. When relevant to the determination of the value of property, a witness may take into account as a basis for his opinion the capitalized value of the reasonable net rental value attributable to the land and existing improvements thereon (as distinguished from the capitalized value of the income or profits attributable to the business conducted thereon).[2]

820. When relevant to the determination of the value of property, a witness may take into account as a basis for his opinion the value of the property or property interest being valued as indicated by the value of the land together with the cost of replacing or reproducing the existing improvements thereon, if the improvements enhance the value of the property or property interest for its highest and best use, less whatever depreciation or obsolescence the improvements have suffered.[2]

821. When relevant to the determination of the value of property, a witness may take into account as a basis for his opinion the nature of the improvements on properties in the general vicinity of the property or property interest being valued and the character of the existing uses being made of such properties.[2]

822. (a) In an eminent domain or inverse condemnation proceeding, notwithstanding the provisions of Sections 814 to 821, inclusive, the following matter is inadmissible as evidence and shall not be taken into account as a basis for an opinion as to the value of property:
(1) The price or other terms and circumstances of an acquisition of prop-

erty or a property interest if the acquisition was for a public use for which the property could have been taken by eminent domain.

The price or other terms and circumstances shall not be excluded pursuant to this paragraph if the proceeding relates to the valuation of all or part of a water system as defined in Section 240 of the Public Utilities Code.

(2) The price at which an offer or option to purchase or lease the property or property interest being valued or any other property was made, or the price at which the property or interest was optioned, offered, or listed for sale or lease, except that an option, offer, or listing may be introduced by a party as an admission of another party to the proceeding; but nothing in this subdivision permits an admission to be used as direct evidence upon any matter that may be shown only by opinion evidence under Section 813.

(3) The value of any property or property interest as assessed for taxation purposes or the amount of taxes which may be due on the property, but nothing in this subdivision prohibits the consideration of actual or estimated taxes for the purpose of determining the reasonable net rental value attributable to the property or property interest being valued.

(4) An opinion as to the value of any property or property interest other than that being valued.

(5) The influence upon the value of the property or property interest being valued of any noncompensable items of value, damage, or injury.

(6) The capitalized value of the income or rental from any property or property interest other than that being valued.

(b) In an action other than an eminent domain or inverse condemnation proceeding, the matters listed in subdivision (a) are not admissible as evidence, and may not be taken into account as a basis for an opinion as to the value of property, except to the extent permitted under the rules of law otherwise applicable.[74]

823. Notwithstanding any other provision of this article, the value of property for which there is no relevant, comparable market may be determined by any method of valuation that is just and equitable.[49]

824. (a) Notwithstanding any other provision of this article, a just and equitable method of determining the value of nonprofit, special use property, as defined by Section 1235.155 of the Code of Civil Procedure, for which there is no relevant, comparable market, is the cost of purchasing land and the reasonable cost of making it suitable for the conduct of the same nonprofit, special use, together with the cost of constructing similar improvements. The method for determining compensation for improvements shall be as set forth in subdivision (b).

(b) Notwithstanding any other provision of this article, a witness providing opinion testimony on the value of nonprofit, special use property, as defined by Section 1235.155 of the Code of Civil Procedure, for which there is no relevant, comparable market, shall base his or her opinion on the value of reproducing the improvements without taking into consideration any depreciation or obsolescence of the improvements.

(c) This section does not apply to actions or proceedings commenced by a public entity or public utility to acquire real property or any interest in real property for the use of water, sewer, electricity, telephone, natural gas, or flood control facilities or rights-of-way where those acquisitions neither require removal or destruction of existing improvements, nor render the property unfit for the owner's present or proposed use.[50]

Article 3: Opinion Testimony on Particular Subjects
Heading of Article 3 renumbered from Article 2 by Stats. 1965, Ch. 1151.

870. A witness may state his opinion as to the sanity of a person when:
(a) The witness is an intimate acquaintance of the person whose sanity is in question;
(b) The witness was a subscribing witness to a writing, the validity of which is in dispute, signed by the person whose sanity is in question and the opinion relates to the sanity of such person at the time the writing was signed; or
(c) The witness is qualified under Section 800 or 801 to testify in the form of an opinion.[1]

DIVISION 8: PRIVILEGES

DIVISION 8 ENACTED BY STATS. 1965, CH. 299.
SECTION 900 - 1070

Chapter 1: Definitions

Chapter 1 enacted by Stats. 1965, Ch. 299.

900. Unless the provision or context otherwise requires, the definitions in this chapter govern the construction of this division. They do not govern the construction of any other division.[1]

901. "Proceeding" means any action, hearing, investigation, inquest, or inquiry (whether conducted by a court, administrative agency, hearing officer, arbitrator, legislative body, or any other person authorized by law) in which, pursuant to law, testimony can be compelled to be given.[1]

902. "Civil proceeding" means any proceeding except a criminal proceeding.[1]

903. "Criminal proceeding" means:
(a) A criminal action; and
(b) A proceeding pursuant to Article 3 (commencing with Section 3060) of Chapter 7 of Division 4 of Title 1 of the Government Code to determine whether a public officer should be removed from office for willful or corrupt misconduct in office.[1]

905. "Presiding officer" means the person authorized to rule on a claim of privilege in the proceeding in which the claim is made.[1]

Chapter 2: Applicability of Division

Chapter 2 enacted by Stats. 1965, Ch. 299.

910. Except as otherwise provided by statute, the provisions of this division apply in all proceedings. The provisions of any statute making rules of evidence inapplicable in particular proceedings, or limiting the applicability of rules of evidence in particular proceedings, do not make this division inapplicable to such proceedings.[1]

Chapter 3: General Provisions Relating to Privileges

Chapter 3 enacted by Stats. 1965, Ch. 299.

911. Except as otherwise provided by statute:
(a) No person has a privilege to refuse to be a witness.
(b) No person has a privilege to refuse to disclose any matter or to refuse to produce any writing, object, or other thing.
(c) No person has a privilege that another shall not be a witness or shall not disclose any matter or shall not produce any writing, object, or other thing.[1]

912. (a) Except as otherwise provided in this section, the right of any person to claim a privilege provided by Section 954 (lawyer-client privilege), 966 (lawyer referral service-client privilege), 980 (privilege for confidential marital communications), 994 (physician-patient privilege), 1014 (psychotherapist-patient privilege), 1033 (privilege of penitent), 1034 (privilege of clergy member), 1035.8 (sexual assault counselor-victim privilege), 1037.5 (domestic violence counselor-victim privilege), or 1038 (human trafficking caseworker-victim privilege) is waived

with respect to a communication protected by the privilege if any holder of the privilege, without coercion, has disclosed a significant part of the communication or has consented to disclosure made by anyone. Consent to disclosure is manifested by any statement or other conduct of the holder of the privilege indicating consent to the disclosure, including failure to claim the privilege in any proceeding in which the holder has legal standing and the opportunity to claim the privilege.
(b) Where two or more persons are joint holders of a privilege provided by Section 954 (lawyer-client privilege), 966 (lawyer referral service-client privilege), 994 (physician-patient privilege), 1014 (psychotherapist-patient privilege), 1035.8 (sexual assault counselor-victim privilege), 1037.5 (domestic violence counselor-victim privilege), or 1038 (human trafficking caseworker-victim privilege), a waiver of the right of a particular joint holder of the privilege to claim the privilege does not affect the right of another joint holder to claim the privilege. In the case of the privilege provided by Section 980 (privilege for confidential marital communications), a waiver of the right of one spouse to claim the privilege does not affect the right of the other spouse to claim the privilege.
(c) A disclosure that is itself privileged is not a waiver of any privilege.
(d) A disclosure in confidence of a communication that is protected by a privilege provided by Section 954 (lawyer-client privilege), 966 (lawyer referral service-client privilege), 994 (physician-patient privilege), 1014 (psychotherapist-patient privilege), 1035.8 (sexual assault counselor-victim privilege), 1037.5 (domestic violence counselor-victim privilege), or 1038 (human trafficking caseworker-victim privilege), when disclosure is reasonably necessary for the accomplishment of the purpose for which the lawyer, lawyer referral service, physician, psychotherapist, sexual assault counselor, domestic violence counselor, or human trafficking caseworker was consulted, is not a waiver of the privilege.[122]

913. (a) If in the instant proceeding or on a prior occasion a privilege is or was exercised not to testify with respect to any matter, or to refuse to disclose or to prevent another from disclosing any matter, neither the presiding officer nor counsel may comment thereon, no presumption shall arise because of the exercise of the privilege, and the trier of fact may not draw any inference therefrom as to the credibility of the witness or as to any matter at issue in the proceeding.
(b) The court, at the request of a party who may be adversely affected because an unfavorable inference may be drawn by the jury because a privilege has been exercised, shall instruct the jury that no presumption arises because of the exercise of the privilege and that the jury may not draw any inference therefrom as to the credibility of the witness or as to any matter at issue in the proceeding.[1]

914. (a) The presiding officer shall determine a claim of privilege in any proceeding in the same manner as a court determines such a claim under Article 2 (commencing with Section 400) of Chapter 4 of Division 3.
(b) No person may be held in contempt for failure to disclose information claimed to be privileged unless

he has failed to comply with an order of a court that he disclose such information. This subdivision does not apply to any governmental agency that has constitutional contempt power, nor does it apply to hearings and investigations of the Industrial Accident Commission, nor does it impliedly repeal Chapter 4 (commencing with Section 9400) of Part 1 of Division 2 of Title 2 of the Government Code. If no other statutory procedure is applicable, the procedure prescribed by Section 1991 of the Code of Civil Procedure shall be followed in seeking an order of a court that the person disclose the information claimed to be privileged.[1]

915. (a) Subject to subdivision (b), the presiding officer may not require disclosure of information claimed to be privileged under this division or attorney work product under subdivision (a) of Section 2018.030 of the Code of Civil Procedure in order to rule on the claim of privilege; provided, however, that in any hearing conducted pursuant to subdivision (c) of Section 1524 of the Penal Code in which a claim of privilege is made and the court determines that there is no other feasible means to rule on the validity of the claim other than to require disclosure, the court shall proceed in accordance with subdivision (b).
(b) When a court is ruling on a claim of privilege under Article 9 (commencing with Section 1040) of Chapter 4 (official information and identity of informer) or under Section 1060 (trade secret) or under subdivision (b) of Section 2018.030 of the Code of Civil Procedure (attorney work product) and is unable to do so without requiring disclosure of the information claimed to be privileged, the court may require the person from whom disclosure is sought or the person authorized to claim the privilege, or both, to disclose the information in chambers out of the presence and hearing of all persons except the person authorized to claim the privilege and any other persons as the person authorized to claim the privilege is willing to have present. If the judge determines that the information is privileged, neither the judge nor any other person may ever disclose, without the consent of a person authorized to permit disclosure, what was disclosed in the course of the proceedings in chambers.[91]

916. (a) The presiding officer, on his own motion or on the motion of any party, shall exclude information that is subject to a claim of privilege under this division if:
(1) The person from whom the information is sought is not a person authorized to claim the privilege; and
(2) There is no party to the proceeding who is a person authorized to claim the privilege.
(b) The presiding officer may not exclude information under this section if:
(1) He is otherwise instructed by a person authorized to permit disclosure; or
(2) The proponent of the evidence establishes that there is no person authorized to claim the privilege in existence.[1]

917. (a) If a privilege is claimed on the ground that the matter sought to be disclosed is a communication made in confidence in the course of the lawyer-client, lawyer referral service-client, physician-patient, psychotherapist-patient, clergy-penitent, marital or domestic partnership, sexual assault

counselor-victim, domestic violence counselor-victim, or human trafficking caseworker-victim relationship, the communication is presumed to have been made in confidence and the opponent of the claim of privilege has the burden of proof to establish that the communication was not confidential.

(b) A communication between persons in a relationship listed in subdivision (a) does not lose its privileged character for the sole reason that it is communicated by electronic means or because persons involved in the delivery, facilitation, or storage of electronic communication may have access to the content of the communication.

(c) For purposes of this section, "electronic" has the same meaning provided in Section 1633.2 of the Civil Code.[127]

918. A party may predicate error on a ruling disallowing a claim of privilege only if he is the holder of the privilege, except that a party may predicate error on a ruling disallowing a claim of privilege by his spouse under Section 970 or 971.[1]

919. (a) Evidence of a statement or other disclosure of privileged information is inadmissible against a holder of the privilege if:

(1) A person authorized to claim the privilege claimed it but nevertheless disclosure erroneously was required to be made; or

(2) The presiding officer did not exclude the privileged information as required by Section 916.

(b) If a person authorized to claim the privilege claimed it, whether in the same or a prior proceeding, but nevertheless disclosure erroneously was required by the presiding officer to be made, neither the failure to refuse to disclose nor the failure to seek review of the order of the presiding officer requiring disclosure indicates consent to the disclosure or constitutes a waiver and, under these circumstances, the disclosure is one made under coercion.[12]

920. Nothing in this division shall be construed to repeal by implication any other statute relating to privileges.[1]

Chapter 4: Particular Privileges

Chapter 4 enacted by Stats. 1965, Ch. 299.

Article 1: Privilege of Defendant in Criminal Case

Article 1 enacted by Stats. 1965, Ch. 299.

930. To the extent that such privilege exists under the Constitution of the United States or the State of California, a defendant in a criminal case has a privilege not to be called as a witness and not to testify.[1]

Article 2: Privilege Against Self-Incrimination

Article 2 enacted by Stats. 1965, Ch. 299.

940. To the extent that such privilege exists under the Constitution of the United States or the State of California, a person has a privilege to refuse to disclose any matter that may tend to incriminate him.[1]

Article 3: Lawyer-Client Privilege

Article 3 enacted by Stats. 1965, Ch. 299.

950. As used in this article, "lawyer" means a person authorized, or reasonably believed by the client to be authorized, to practice law in any state or nation.[1]

951. As used in this article, "client" means a person who, directly or through an authorized representative, consults a lawyer for the purpose of retaining the lawyer or securing legal service or advice from him in his professional capacity, and includes an incompetent (a) who himself so consults the lawyer or (b) whose guardian or conservator so consults the lawyer in behalf of the incompetent.[1]

952. As used in this article, "confidential communication between client and lawyer" means information transmitted between a client and his or her lawyer in the course of that relationship and in confidence by a means which, so far as the client is aware, discloses the information to no third persons other than those who are present to further the interest of the client in the consultation or those to whom disclosure is reasonably necessary for the transmission of the information or the accomplishment of the purpose for which the lawyer is consulted, and includes a legal opinion formed and the advice given by the lawyer in the course of that relationship.[78]

953. As used in this article, "holder of the privilege" means:

(a) The client, if the client has no guardian or conservator.

(b) (1) A guardian or conservator of the client, if the client has a guardian or conservator, except as provided in paragraph (2).

(2) If the guardian or conservator has an actual or apparent conflict of interest with the client, then the guardian or conservator does not hold the privilege.

(c) The personal representative of the client if the client is dead, including a personal representative appointed pursuant to Section 12252 of the Probate Code.

(d) A successor, assign, trustee in dissolution, or any similar representative of a firm, association, organization, partnership, business trust, corporation, or public entity that is no longer in existence.[149]

954. Subject to Section 912 and except as otherwise provided in this article, the client, whether or not a party, has a privilege to refuse to disclose, and to prevent another from disclosing, a confidential communication between client and lawyer if the privilege is claimed by:

(a) The holder of the privilege;

(b) A person who is authorized to claim the privilege by the holder of the privilege; or

(c) The person who was the lawyer at the time of the confidential communication, but such person may not claim the privilege if there is no holder of the privilege in existence or if he is otherwise instructed by a person authorized to permit disclosure.

The relationship of attorney and client shall exist between a law corporation as defined in Article 10 (commencing with Section 6160) of Chapter 4 of Division 3 of the Business and Professions Code and the persons to whom it renders professional services, as well as between such persons and members of the State Bar employed by such corporation to render services to such persons. The word "persons" as used in this subdivision includes partnerships, corporations, limited liability companies, associations and other groups and entities.[55]

955. The lawyer who received or made

a communication subject to the privilege under this article shall claim the privilege whenever he is present when the communication is sought to be disclosed and is authorized to claim the privilege under subdivision (c) of Section 954.[1]

956. (a) There is no privilege under this article if the services of the lawyer were sought or obtained to enable or aid anyone to commit or plan to commit a crime or a fraud.
(b) This exception to the privilege granted by this article shall not apply to legal services rendered in compliance with state and local laws on medicinal cannabis or adult-use cannabis, and confidential communications provided for the purpose of rendering those services are confidential communications between client and lawyer, as defined in Section 952, provided the lawyer also advises the client on conflicts with respect to federal law.[138]

956.5. There is no privilege under this article if the lawyer reasonably believes that disclosure of any confidential communication relating to representation of a client is necessary to prevent a criminal act that the lawyer reasonably believes is likely to result in the death of, or substantial bodily harm to, an individual.[94]

957. There is no privilege under this article as to a communication relevant to an issue between parties all of whom claim through a deceased client, regardless of whether the claims are by testate or intestate succession, nonprobate transfer, or inter vivos transaction.[106]

958. There is no privilege under this article as to a communication relevant to an issue of breach, by the lawyer or by the client, of a duty arising out of the lawyer-client relationship.[1]

959. There is no privilege under this article as to a communication relevant to an issue concerning the intention or competence of a client executing an attested document of which the lawyer is an attesting witness, or concerning the execution or attestation of such a document.[1]

960. There is no privilege under this article as to a communication relevant to an issue concerning the intention of a client, now deceased, with respect to a deed of conveyance, will, or other writing, executed by the client, purporting to affect an interest in property.[1]

961. There is no privilege under this article as to a communication relevant to an issue concerning the validity of a deed of conveyance, will, or other writing, executed by a client, now deceased, purporting to affect an interest in property.[1]

962. Where two or more clients have retained or consulted a lawyer upon a matter of common interest, none of them, nor the successor in interest of any of them, may claim a privilege under this article as to a communication made in the course of that relationship when such communication is offered in a civil proceeding between one of such clients (or his successor in interest) and another of such clients (or his successor in interest).[1]

Article 3.5: Lawyer Referral Service-Client Privilege
Article 3.5 added by Stats. 2013, Ch. 123, Sec. 2.

965. For purposes of this article, the

following terms have the following meanings:

(a) "Client" means a person who, directly or through an authorized representative, consults a lawyer referral service for the purpose of retaining, or securing legal services or advice from, a lawyer in his or her professional capacity, and includes an incompetent who consults the lawyer referral service himself or herself or whose guardian or conservator consults the lawyer referral service on his or her behalf.

(b) "Confidential communication between client and lawyer referral service" means information transmitted between a client and a lawyer referral service in the course of that relationship and in confidence by a means that, so far as the client is aware, does not disclose the information to third persons other than those who are present to further the interests of the client in the consultation or those to whom disclosure is reasonably necessary for the transmission of the information or the accomplishment of the purpose for which the lawyer referral service is consulted.

(c) "Holder of the privilege" means any of the following:

(1) The client, if the client has no guardian or conservator.

(2) A guardian or conservator of the client, if the client has a guardian or conservator.

(3) The personal representative of the client if the client is dead, including a personal representative appointed pursuant to Section 12252 of the Probate Code.

(4) A successor, assign, trustee in dissolution, or any similar representative of a firm, association, organization, partnership, business trust, corporation, or public entity that is no longer in existence.

(d) "Lawyer referral service" means a lawyer referral service certified under, and operating in compliance with, Section 6155 of the Business and Professions Code or an enterprise reasonably believed by the client to be a lawyer referral service certified under, and operating in compliance with, Section 6155 of the Business and Professions Code.[119]

966. (a) Subject to Section 912 and except as otherwise provided in this article, the client, whether or not a party, has a privilege to refuse to disclose, and to prevent another from disclosing, a confidential communication between client and lawyer referral service if the privilege is claimed by any of the following:

(1) The holder of the privilege.

(2) A person who is authorized to claim the privilege by the holder of the privilege.

(3) The lawyer referral service or a staff person thereof, but the lawyer referral service or a staff person thereof may not claim the privilege if there is no holder of the privilege in existence or if the lawyer referral service or a staff person thereof is otherwise instructed by a person authorized to permit disclosure.

(b) The relationship of lawyer referral service and client shall exist between a lawyer referral service, as defined in Section 965, and the persons to whom it renders services, as well as between such persons and anyone employed by the lawyer referral service to render services to such persons. The word "persons" as used in this subdivision includes partnerships, corporations, limited liability companies, associations, and other groups and entities.[119]

967. A lawyer referral service that has received or made a communication subject to the privilege under this article shall claim the privilege if the communication is sought to be disclosed and the client has not consented to the disclosure.[119]

968. There is no privilege under this article if either of the following applies:
(a) The services of the lawyer referral service were sought or obtained to enable or aid anyone to commit or plan to commit a crime or a fraud.
(b) A staff person of the lawyer referral service who receives a confidential communication in processing a request for legal assistance reasonably believes that disclosure of the confidential communication is necessary to prevent a criminal act that the staff person of the lawyer referral service reasonably believes is likely to result in the death of, or substantial bodily harm to, an individual.[119]

Article 4: Privilege Not to Testify Against Spouse

Article 4 enacted by Stats. 1965, Ch. 299.

970. Except as otherwise provided by statute, a married person has a privilege not to testify against his spouse in any proceeding.[1]

971. Except as otherwise provided by statute, a married person whose spouse is a party to a proceeding has a privilege not to be called as a witness by an adverse party to that proceeding without the prior express consent of the spouse having the privilege under this section unless the party calling the spouse does so in good faith without knowledge of the marital relationship.[1]

972. A married person does not have a privilege under this article in:
(a) A proceeding brought by or on behalf of one spouse against the other spouse.
(b) A proceeding to commit or otherwise place his or her spouse or his or her spouse's property, or both, under the control of another because of the spouse's alleged mental or physical condition.
(c) A proceeding brought by or on behalf of a spouse to establish his or her competence.
(d) A proceeding under the Juvenile Court Law, Chapter 2 (commencing with Section 200) of Part 1 of Division 2 of the Welfare and Institutions Code.
(e) A criminal proceeding in which one spouse is charged with:
 (1) A crime against the person or property of the other spouse or of a child, parent, relative, or cohabitant of either, whether committed before or during marriage.
 (2) A crime against the person or property of a third person committed in the course of committing a crime against the person or property of the other spouse, whether committed before or during marriage.
 (3) Bigamy.
 (4) A crime defined by Section 270 or 270a of the Penal Code.
(f) A proceeding resulting from a criminal act which occurred prior to legal marriage of the spouses to each other regarding knowledge acquired prior to that marriage if prior to the legal marriage the witness spouse was aware that his or her spouse had been arrested for or had been formally charged with the crime or crimes about which the spouse is called to testify.

(g) A proceeding brought against the spouse by a former spouse so long as the property and debts of the marriage have not been adjudicated, or in order to establish, modify, or enforce a child, family or spousal support obligation arising from the marriage to the former spouse; in a proceeding brought against a spouse by the other parent in order to establish, modify, or enforce a child support obligation for a child of a nonmarital relationship of the spouse; or in a proceeding brought against a spouse by the guardian of a child of that spouse in order to establish, modify, or enforce a child support obligation of the spouse. The married person does not have a privilege under this subdivision to refuse to provide information relating to the issues of income, expenses, assets, debts, and employment of either spouse, but may assert the privilege as otherwise provided in this article if other information is requested by the former spouse, guardian, or other parent of the child.

Any person demanding the otherwise privileged information made available by this subdivision, who also has an obligation to support the child for whom an order to establish, modify, or enforce child support is sought, waives his or her marital privilege to the same extent as the spouse as provided in this subdivision.[44]

973. (a) Unless erroneously compelled to do so, a married person who testifies in a proceeding to which his spouse is a party, or who testifies against his spouse in any proceeding, does not have a privilege under this article in the proceeding in which such testimony is given.

(b) There is no privilege under this article in a civil proceeding brought or defended by a married person for the immediate benefit of his spouse or of himself and his spouse.[1]

Article 5: Privilege for Confidential Marital Communications
Article 5 enacted by Stats. 1965, Ch. 299.

980. Subject to Section 912 and except as otherwise provided in this article, a spouse (or his or her guardian or conservator when he or she has a guardian or conservator), whether or not a party, has a privilege during the marital or domestic partnership relationship and afterwards to refuse to disclose, and to prevent another from disclosing, a communication if he or she claims the privilege and the communication was made in confidence between him or her and the other spouse while they were spouses.[128]

981. There is no privilege under this article if the communication was made, in whole or in part, to enable or aid anyone to commit or plan to commit a crime or a fraud.[1]

982. There is no privilege under this article in a proceeding to commit either spouse or otherwise place him or his property, or both, under the control of another because of his alleged mental or physical condition.[1]

983. There is no privilege under this article in a proceeding brought by or on behalf of either spouse to establish his competence.[1]

984. There is no privilege under this article in:

(a) A proceeding brought by or on behalf of one spouse against the other spouse.

(b) A proceeding between a surviving spouse and a person who claims through the deceased spouse, regardless of whether such claim is by testate or intestate succession or by inter vivos transaction.[1]

985. There is no privilege under this article in a criminal proceeding in which one spouse is charged with:
(a) A crime committed at any time against the person or property of the other spouse or of a child of either.
(b) A crime committed at any time against the person or property of a third person committed in the course of committing a crime against the person or property of the other spouse.
(c) Bigamy.
(d) A crime defined by Section 270 or 270a of the Penal Code.[14]

986. There is no privilege under this article in a proceeding under the Juvenile Court Law, Chapter 2 (commencing with Section 200) of Part 1 of Division 2 of the Welfare and Institutions Code.[26]

987. There is no privilege under this article in a criminal proceeding in which the communication is offered in evidence by a defendant who is one of the spouses between whom the communication was made.[1]

Article 6: Physician-Patient Privilege
Article 6 enacted by Stats. 1965, Ch. 299.

990. As used in this article, "physician" means a person authorized, or reasonably believed by the patient to be authorized, to practice medicine in any state or nation.[1]

991. As used in this article, "patient" means a person who consults a physician or submits to an examination by a physician for the purpose of securing a diagnosis or preventive, palliative, or curative treatment of his physical or mental or emotional condition.[1]

992. As used in this article, "confidential communication between patient and physician" means information, including information obtained by an examination of the patient, transmitted between a patient and his physician in the course of that relationship and in confidence by a means which, so far as the patient is aware, discloses the information to no third persons other than those who are present to further the interest of the patient in the consultation or those to whom disclosure is reasonably necessary for the transmission of the information or the accomplishment of the purpose for which the physician is consulted, and includes a diagnosis made and the advice given by the physician in the course of that relationship.[4]

993. As used in this article, "holder of the privilege" means:
(a) The patient when he has no guardian or conservator.
(b) A guardian or conservator of the patient when the patient has a guardian or conservator.
(c) The personal representative of the patient if the patient is dead.[1]

994. Subject to Section 912 and except as otherwise provided in this article, the patient, whether or not a party, has a privilege to refuse to disclose, and to prevent another from disclosing, a confidential communication between patient and physician if the privilege is claimed by:
(a) The holder of the privilege;
(b) A person who is authorized to claim the privilege by the holder of the privilege; or

(c) The person who was the physician at the time of the confidential communication, but such person may not claim the privilege if there is no holder of the privilege in existence or if he or she is otherwise instructed by a person authorized to permit disclosure.
The relationship of a physician and patient shall exist between a medical or podiatry corporation as defined in the Medical Practice Act and the patient to whom it renders professional services, as well as between such patients and licensed physicians and surgeons employed by such corporation to render services to such patients. The word "persons" as used in this subdivision includes partnerships, corporations, limited liability companies, associations, and other groups and entities.[56]

995. The physician who received or made a communication subject to the privilege under this article shall claim the privilege whenever he is present when the communication is sought to be disclosed and is authorized to claim the privilege under subdivision (c) of Section 994.[1]

996. There is no privilege under this article as to a communication relevant to an issue concerning the condition of the patient if such issue has been tendered by:
(a) The patient;
(b) Any party claiming through or under the patient;
(c) Any party claiming as a beneficiary of the patient through a contract to which the patient is or was a party; or
(d) The plaintiff in an action brought under Section 376 or 377 of the Code of Civil Procedure for damages for the injury or death of the patient.[1]

997. There is no privilege under this article if the services of the physician were sought or obtained to enable or aid anyone to commit or plan to commit a crime or a tort or to escape detection or apprehension after the commission of a crime or a tort.[1]

998. There is no privilege under this article in a criminal proceeding.[1]

999. There is no privilege under this article as to a communication relevant to an issue concerning the condition of the patient in a proceeding to recover damages on account of the conduct of the patient if good cause for disclosure of the communication is shown.[15]

1000. There is no privilege under this article as to a communication relevant to an issue between parties all of whom claim through a deceased patient, regardless of whether the claims are by testate or intestate succession or by inter vivos transaction.[1]

1001. There is no privilege under this article as to a communication relevant to an issue of breach, by the physician or by the patient, of a duty arising out of the physician-patient relationship.[1]

1002. There is no privilege under this article as to a communication relevant to an issue concerning the intention of a patient, now deceased, with respect to a deed of conveyance, will, or other writing, executed by the patient, purporting to affect an interest in property.[1]

1003. There is no privilege under this article as to a communication relevant to an issue concerning the validity of a deed of conveyance, will, or other writing, executed by a patient, now deceased, purporting to affect an interest in property.[1]

1004. There is no privilege under this article in a proceeding to commit the patient or otherwise place him or his property, or both, under the control of another because of his alleged mental or physical condition.[1]

1005. There is no privilege under this article in a proceeding brought by or on behalf of the patient to establish his competence.[1]

1006. There is no privilege under this article as to information that the physician or the patient is required to report to a public employee, or as to information required to be recorded in a public office, if such report or record is open to public inspection.[1]

1007. There is no privilege under this article in a proceeding brought by a public entity to determine whether a right, authority, license, or privilege (including the right or privilege to be employed by the public entity or to hold a public office) should be revoked, suspended, terminated, limited, or conditioned.[1]

Article 7: Psychotherapist-Patient Privilege
Article 7 enacted by Stats. 1965, Ch. 299.

1010. As used in this article, "psychotherapist" means a person who is, or is reasonably believed by the patient to be:
(a) A person authorized to practice medicine in any state or nation who devotes, or is reasonably believed by the patient to devote, a substantial portion of their time to the practice of psychiatry.
(b) A person licensed as a psychologist under Chapter 6.6 (commencing with Section 2900) of Division 2 of the Business and Professions Code.
(c) A person licensed as a clinical social worker under Chapter 14 (commencing with Section 4991) of Division 2 of the Business and Professions Code, when they are engaged in applied psychotherapy of a nonmedical nature.
(d) A person who is serving as a school psychologist and holds a credential authorizing that service issued by the state.
(e) A person licensed as a marriage and family therapist under Chapter 13 (commencing with Section 4980) of Division 2 of the Business and Professions Code.
(f) A person registered as a registered psychological associate who is under the supervision of a licensed psychologist as required by Section 2913 of the Business and Professions Code, or a person registered as an associate marriage and family therapist who is under the supervision of a licensed marriage and family therapist, a licensed clinical social worker, a licensed professional clinical counselor, a licensed psychologist, or a licensed physician and surgeon certified in psychiatry, as specified in Section 4980.44 of the Business and Professions Code.
(g) A person registered as an associate clinical social worker who is under supervision as specified in Section 4996.23 of the Business and Professions Code.
(h) A psychological intern as defined in Section 2911 of the Business and Professions Code who is under the primary supervision of a licensed psychologist.
(i) A trainee, as defined in subdivision (c) of Section 4980.03 of the Business and Professions Code, who is fulfilling

their supervised practicum required by subparagraph (B) of paragraph (1) of subdivision (d) of Section 4980.36 of, or subdivision (c) of Section 4980.37 of, the Business and Professions Code and is supervised by a licensed psychologist, a board certified psychiatrist, a licensed clinical social worker, a licensed marriage and family therapist, or a licensed professional clinical counselor.

(j) A person licensed as a registered nurse pursuant to Chapter 6 (commencing with Section 2700) of Division 2 of the Business and Professions Code, who possesses a master's degree in psychiatric-mental health nursing and is listed as a psychiatric-mental health nurse by the Board of Registered Nursing.

(k) An advanced practice registered nurse who is certified as a clinical nurse specialist pursuant to Article 9 (commencing with Section 2838) of Chapter 6 of Division 2 of the Business and Professions Code and who participates in expert clinical practice in the specialty of psychiatric-mental health nursing.

(l) A person rendering mental health treatment or counseling services as authorized pursuant to Section 6924 of the Family Code.

(m) A person licensed as a professional clinical counselor under Chapter 16 (commencing with Section 4999.10) of Division 2 of the Business and Professions Code.

(n) A person registered as an associate professional clinical counselor who is under the supervision of a licensed professional clinical counselor, a licensed marriage and family therapist, a licensed clinical social worker, a licensed psychologist, or a licensed physician and surgeon certified in psychiatry, as specified in Sections 4999.42 to 4999.48, inclusive, of the Business and Professions Code.

(o) A clinical counselor trainee, as defined in subdivision (g) of Section 4999.12 of the Business and Professions Code, who is fulfilling their supervised practicum required by paragraph (3) of subdivision (c) of Section 4999.32 of, or paragraph (3) of subdivision (c) of Section 4999.33 of, the Business and Professions Code, and is supervised by a licensed psychologist, a board-certified psychiatrist, a licensed clinical social worker, a licensed marriage and family therapist, or a licensed professional clinical counselor.[163]

1010.5. A communication between a patient and an educational psychologist, licensed under Chapter 13.5 (commencing with Section 4989.10) of Division 2 of the Business and Professions Code, shall be privileged to the same extent, and subject to the same limitations, as a communication between a patient and a psychotherapist described in subdivisions (c), (d), and (e) of Section 1010.[157]

1011. As used in this article, "patient" means a person who consults a psychotherapist or submits to an examination by a psychotherapist for the purpose of securing a diagnosis or preventive, palliative, or curative treatment of his mental or emotional condition or who submits to an examination of his mental or emotional condition for the purpose of scientific research on mental or emotional problems.[1]

1012. As used in this article, "confidential communication between patient and psychotherapist" means information, including information obtained by an examination of the patient, transmitted between a patient and his psychotherapist in the course of that relationship and in confidence by a means which, so far as the patient is aware, discloses the information to no third persons other than those who are present to further the interest of the patient in the consultation, or those to whom disclosure is reasonably necessary for the transmission of the information or the accomplishment of the purpose for which the psychotherapist is consulted, and includes a diagnosis made and the advice given by the psychotherapist in the course of that relationship.[11]

1013. As used in this article, "holder of the privilege" means:
(a) The patient when he has no guardian or conservator.
(b) A guardian or conservator of the patient when the patient has a guardian or conservator.
(c) The personal representative of the patient if the patient is dead.[1]

1014. Subject to Section 912 and except as otherwise provided in this article, the patient, whether or not a party, has a privilege to refuse to disclose, and to prevent another from disclosing, a confidential communication between patient and psychotherapist if the privilege is claimed by:
(a) The holder of the privilege.
(b) A person who is authorized to claim the privilege by the holder of the privilege.
(c) The person who was the psychotherapist at the time of the confidential communication, but the person may not claim the privilege if there is no holder of the privilege in existence or if he or she is otherwise instructed by a person authorized to permit disclosure.
The relationship of a psychotherapist and patient shall exist between a psychological corporation as defined in Article 9 (commencing with Section 2995) of Chapter 6.6 of Division 2 of the Business and Professions Code, a marriage and family therapist corporation as defined in Article 6 (commencing with Section 4987.5) of Chapter 13 of Division 2 of the Business and Professions Code, a licensed clinical social workers corporation as defined in Article 5 (commencing with Section 4998) of Chapter 14 of Division 2 of the Business and Professions Code, or a professional clinical counselor corporation as defined in Article 7 (commencing with Section 4999.123) of Chapter 16 of Division 2 of the Business and Professions Code, and the patient to whom it renders professional services, as well as between those patients and psychotherapists employed by those corporations to render services to those patients. The word "persons" as used in this subdivision includes partnerships, corporations, limited liability companies, associations, and other groups and entities.[112]

1015. The psychotherapist who received or made a communication subject to the privilege under this article shall claim the privilege whenever he is present when the communication is sought to be disclosed and is authorized to claim the privilege under subdivision (c) of Section 1014.[1]

1016. There is no privilege under this article as to a communication relevant

to an issue concerning the mental or emotional condition of the patient if such issue has been tendered by:
(a) The patient;
(b) Any party claiming through or under the patient;
(c) Any party claiming as a beneficiary of the patient through a contract to which the patient is or was a party; or
(d) The plaintiff in an action brought under Section 376 or 377 of the Code of Civil Procedure for damages for the injury or death of the patient.[1]

1017. (a) There is no privilege under this article if the psychotherapist is appointed by order of a court to examine the patient, but this exception does not apply where the psychotherapist is appointed by order of the court upon the request of the lawyer for the defendant in a criminal proceeding in order to provide the lawyer with information needed so that he or she may advise the defendant whether to enter or withdraw a plea based on insanity or to present a defense based on his or her mental or emotional condition.
(b) There is no privilege under this article if the psychotherapist is appointed by the Board of Prison Terms to examine a patient pursuant to the provisions of Article 4 (commencing with Section 2960) of Chapter 7 of Title 1 of Part 3 of the Penal Code.[40]

1018. There is no privilege under this article if the services of the psychotherapist were sought or obtained to enable or aid anyone to commit or plan to commit a crime or a tort or to escape detection or apprehension after the commission of a crime or a tort.[1]

1019. There is no privilege under this article as to a communication relevant to an issue between parties all of whom claim through a deceased patient, regardless of whether the claims are by testate or intestate succession or by inter vivos transaction.[1]

1020. There is no privilege under this article as to a communication relevant to an issue of breach, by the psychotherapist or by the patient, of a duty arising out of the psychotherapist-patient relationship.[1]

1021. There is no privilege under this article as to a communication relevant to an issue concerning the intention of a patient, now deceased, with respect to a deed of conveyance, will, or other writing, executed by the patient, purporting to affect an interest in property.[1]

1022. There is no privilege under this article as to a communication relevant to an issue concerning the validity of a deed of conveyance, will, or other writing, executed by a patient, now deceased, purporting to affect an interest in property.[1]

1023. There is no privilege under this article in a proceeding under Chapter 6 (commencing with Section 1367) of Title 10 of Part 2 of the Penal Code initiated at the request of the defendant in a criminal action to determine his sanity.[1]

1024. There is no privilege under this article if the psychotherapist has reasonable cause to believe that the patient is in such mental or emotional condition as to be dangerous to himself or to the person or property of another and that disclosure of the communication is necessary to prevent the threatened danger.[1]

1025. There is no privilege under this

article in a proceeding brought by or on behalf of the patient to establish his competence.[1]

1026. There is no privilege under this article as to information that the psychotherapist or the patient is required to report to a public employee or as to information required to be recorded in a public office, if such report or record is open to public inspection.[1]

1027. There is no privilege under this article if all of the following circumstances exist:
(a) The patient is a child under the age of 16.
(b) The psychotherapist has reasonable cause to believe that the patient has been the victim of a crime and that disclosure of the communication is in the best interest of the child.[10]

Article 8: Clergy Penitent Privileges
Heading of Article 8 amended by Stats. 2002, Ch. 806, Sec. 18.

1030. As used in this article, a "member of the clergy" means a priest, minister, religious practitioner, or similar functionary of a church or of a religious denomination or religious organization.[84]

1031. As used in this article, "penitent" means a person who has made a penitential communication to a member of the clergy.[85]

1032. As used in this article, "penitential communication" means a communication made in confidence, in the presence of no third person so far as the penitent is aware, to a member of the clergy who, in the course of the discipline or practice of the clergy member's church, denomination, or organization, is authorized or accustomed to hear those communications and, under the discipline or tenets of his or her church, denomination, or organization, has a duty to keep those communications secret.[86]

1033. Subject to Section 912, a penitent, whether or not a party, has a privilege to refuse to disclose, and to prevent another from disclosing, a penitential communication if he or she claims the privilege.[87]

1034. Subject to Section 912, a member of the clergy, whether or not a party, has a privilege to refuse to disclose a penitential communication if he or she claims the privilege.[88]

Article 8.5: Sexual Assault Counselor-Victim Privilege
Heading of Article 8.5 amended by Stats. 2006, Ch. 689, Sec. 3.

1035. As used in this article, "victim" means a person who consults a sexual assault counselor for the purpose of securing advice or assistance concerning a mental, physical, or emotional condition caused by a sexual assault.[99]

1035.2. As used in this article, "sexual assault counselor" means any of the following:
(a) A person who is engaged in any office, hospital, institution, or center commonly known as a rape crisis center, whose primary purpose is the rendering of advice or assistance to victims of sexual assault and who has received a certificate evidencing completion of a training program in the counseling of sexual assault victims issued by a counseling center that meets the criteria for the award of a grant established pursuant to Section 13837 of the

Penal Code and who meets one of the following requirements:

(1) Is a psychotherapist as defined in Section 1010; has a master's degree in counseling or a related field; or has one year of counseling experience, at least six months of which is in rape crisis counseling.

(2) Has 40 hours of training as described below and is supervised by an individual who qualifies as a counselor under paragraph (1). The training, supervised by a person qualified under paragraph (1), shall include, but not be limited to, the following areas:

(A) Law.

(B) Medicine.

(C) Societal attitudes.

(D) Crisis intervention and counseling techniques.

(E) Role playing.

(F) Referral services.

(G) Sexuality.

(b) A person who is engaged in a program on the campus of a public or private institution of higher education, whose primary purpose is the rendering of advice or assistance to victims of sexual assault and who has received a certificate evidencing completion of a training program in the counseling of sexual assault victims issued by a counseling center that meets the criteria for the award of a grant established pursuant to Section 13837 of the Penal Code and who meets one of the following requirements:

(1) Is a psychotherapist as defined in Section 1010; has a master's degree in counseling or a related field; or has one year of counseling experience, at least six months of which is in rape crisis counseling.

(2) Has 40 hours of training as described below and is supervised by an individual who qualifies as a counselor under paragraph (1). The training, supervised by a person qualified under paragraph (1), shall include, but not be limited to, the following areas:

(A) Law.

(B) Medicine.

(C) Societal attitudes.

(D) Crisis intervention and counseling techniques.

(E) Role playing.

(F) Referral services.

(G) Sexuality.

(c) A person who is employed by any organization providing the programs specified in Section 13835.2 of the Penal Code, whether financially compensated or not, for the purpose of counseling and assisting sexual assault victims, and who meets one of the following requirements:

(1) Is a psychotherapist as defined in Section 1010; has a master's degree in counseling or a related field; or has one year of counseling experience, at least six months of which is in rape assault counseling.

(2) Has the minimum training for sexual assault counseling required by guidelines established by the employing agency pursuant to subdivision (c) of Section 13835.10 of the Penal Code, and is supervised by an individual who qualifies as a counselor under paragraph (1). The training, supervised by a person qualified under paragraph (1), shall include, but not be limited to, the following areas:

(A) Law.

(B) Victimology.

(C) Counseling.

(D) Client and system advocacy.

(E) Referral services.[143]

1035.4. As used in this article, "confidential communication between the sexual assault counselor and the victim" means information transmitted between the victim and the sexual assault counselor in the course of their relationship and in confidence by a means which, so far as the victim is aware, discloses the information to no third persons other than those who are present to further the interests of the victim in the consultation or those to whom disclosures are reasonably necessary for the transmission of the information or an accomplishment of the purposes for which the sexual assault counselor is consulted. The term includes all information regarding the facts and circumstances involving the alleged sexual assault and also includes all information regarding the victim's prior or subsequent sexual conduct, and opinions regarding the victim's sexual conduct or reputation in sexual matters.

The court may compel disclosure of information received by the sexual assault counselor which constitutes relevant evidence of the facts and circumstances involving an alleged sexual assault about which the victim is complaining and which is the subject of a criminal proceeding if the court determines that the probative value outweighs the effect on the victim, the treatment relationship, and the treatment services if disclosure is compelled. The court may also compel disclosure in proceedings related to child abuse if the court determines the probative value outweighs the effect on the victim, the treatment relationship, and the treatment services if disclosure is compelled.

When a court is ruling on a claim of privilege under this article, the court may require the person from whom disclosure is sought or the person authorized to claim the privilege, or both, to disclose the information in chambers out of the presence and hearing of all persons except the person authorized to claim the privilege and such other persons as the person authorized to claim the privilege is willing to have present. If the judge determines that the information is privileged and must not be disclosed, neither he or she nor any other person may ever disclose, without the consent of a person authorized to permit disclosure, what was disclosed in the course of the proceedings in chambers.

If the court determines certain information shall be disclosed, the court shall so order and inform the defendant. If the court finds there is a reasonable likelihood that particular information is subject to disclosure pursuant to the balancing test provided in this section, the following procedure shall be followed:

(1) The court shall inform the defendant of the nature of the information which may be subject to disclosure.

(2) The court shall order a hearing out of the presence of the jury, if any, and at the hearing allow the questioning of the sexual assault counselor regarding the information which the court has determined may be subject to disclosure.

(3) At the conclusion of the hearing, the court shall rule which items of information, if any, shall be disclosed. The court may make an order stating what evidence may be introduced by the defendant and the nature of questions to be permitted. The defendant may then offer evidence pursuant to the order of the court. Admission of

evidence concerning the sexual conduct of the complaining witness is subject to Sections 352, 782, and 1103.[31]

1035.6. As used in this article, "holder of the privilege" means:
(a) The victim when such person has no guardian or conservator.
(b) A guardian or conservator of the victim when the victim has a guardian or conservator.
(c) The personal representative of the victim if the victim is dead.[24]

1035.8. A victim of a sexual assault, whether or not a party, has a privilege to refuse to disclose, and to prevent another from disclosing, a confidential communication between the victim and a sexual assault counselor if the privilege is claimed by any of the following :
(a) The holder of the privilege;
(b) A person who is authorized to claim the privilege by the holder of the privilege; or
(c) The person who was the sexual assault counselor at the time of the confidential communication, but that person may not claim the privilege if there is no holder of the privilege in existence or if he or she is otherwise instructed by a person authorized to permit disclosure.[100]

1036. The sexual assault counselor who received or made a communication subject to the privilege under this article shall claim the privilege if he or she is present when the communication is sought to be disclosed and is authorized to claim the privilege under subdivision (c) of Section 1035.8.[101]

1036.2. As used in this article, "sexual assault" includes all of the following:
(a) Rape, as defined in Section 261 of the Penal Code.
(b) Unlawful sexual intercourse, as defined in Section 261.5 of the Penal Code.
(c) Rape in concert with force and violence, as defined in Section 264.1 of the Penal Code.
(d) Sodomy, as defined in Section 286 of the Penal Code, except a violation of subdivision (e) of that section.
(e) A violation of Section 288 of the Penal Code.
(f) Oral copulation, as defined in Section 287 of, or former Section 288a of, the Penal Code, except a violation of subdivision (e) of those sections.
(g) Sexual penetration, as defined in Section 289 of the Penal Code.
(h) Annoying or molesting a child under 18 years of age, as defined in Section 647a of the Penal Code.
(i) Any attempt to commit any of the acts listed in this section.[162]

Article 8.7: Domestic Violence Counselor-Victim Privilege
Heading of Article 8.7 amended by Stats. 2006, Ch. 689, Sec. 8.

1037. As used in this article, "victim" means any person who suffers domestic violence, as defined in Section 1037.7.[37]

1037.1. (a) (1) As used in this article, "domestic violence counselor" means a person who is employed by a domestic violence victim service organization, as defined in this article, whether financially compensated or not, for the purpose of rendering advice or assistance to victims of domestic violence and who has at least 40 hours of training as specified in paragraph (2).
(2) The 40 hours of training shall be

supervised by an individual who qualifies as a counselor under paragraph (1), and who has at least one year of experience counseling domestic violence victims for the domestic violence victim service organization. The training shall include, but need not be limited to, the following areas: history of domestic violence, civil and criminal law as it relates to domestic violence, the domestic violence victim-counselor privilege and other laws that protect the confidentiality of victim records and information, societal attitudes towards domestic violence, peer counseling techniques, housing, public assistance and other financial resources available to meet the financial needs of domestic violence victims, and referral services available to domestic violence victims.

(3) A domestic violence counselor who has been employed by the domestic violence victim service organization for a period of less than six months shall be supervised by a domestic violence counselor who has at least one year of experience counseling domestic violence victims for the domestic violence victim service organization.

(b) As used in this article, "domestic violence victim service organization" means either of the following:

(1) A nongovernmental organization or entity that provides shelter, programs, or services to victims of domestic violence and their children, including, but not limited to, either of the following:

(A) Domestic violence shelter-based programs, as described in Section 18294 of the Welfare and Institutions Code.

(B) Other programs with the primary mission to provide services to victims of domestic violence whether or not that program exists in an agency that provides additional services.

(2) Programs on the campus of a public or private institution of higher education with the primary mission to provide support or advocacy services to victims of domestic violence.[135]

1037.2. (a) As used in this article, "confidential communication" means any information, including, but not limited to, written or oral communication, transmitted between the victim and the counselor in the course of their relationship and in confidence by a means which, so far as the victim is aware, discloses the information to no third persons other than those who are present to further the interests of the victim in the consultation or those to whom disclosures are reasonably necessary for the transmission of the information or an accomplishment of the purposes for which the domestic violence counselor is consulted. The term includes all information regarding the facts and circumstances involving all incidences of domestic violence, as well as all information about the children of the victim or abuser and the relationship of the victim with the abuser.

(b) The court may compel disclosure of information received by a domestic violence counselor which constitutes relevant evidence of the facts and circumstances involving a crime allegedly perpetrated against the victim or another household member and which is the subject of a criminal proceeding, if the court determines that the probative value of the information outweighs the effect of disclosure of the information on the victim, the counseling relationship, and the counseling services. The court may compel disclosure if the victim is either dead or not the complaining witness in a criminal action against the perpetrator. The court may also compel disclosure in proceedings related to child abuse if the court determines that the probative value of the evidence outweighs the effect of the disclosure on the victim, the counseling relationship, and the counseling services.

(c) When a court rules on a claim of privilege under this article, it may require the person from whom disclosure is sought or the person authorized to claim the privilege, or both, to disclose the information in chambers out of the presence and hearing of all persons except the person authorized to claim the privilege and such other persons as the person authorized to claim the privilege consents to have present. If the judge determines that the information is privileged and shall not be disclosed, neither he nor she nor any other person may disclose, without the consent of a person authorized to permit disclosure, any information disclosed in the course of the proceedings in chambers.

(d) If the court determines that information shall be disclosed, the court shall so order and inform the defendant in the criminal action. If the court finds there is a reasonable likelihood that any information is subject to disclosure pursuant to the balancing test provided in this section, the procedure specified in subdivisions (1), (2), and (3) of Section 1035.4 shall be followed.[103]

1037.3. Nothing in this article shall be construed to limit any obligation to report instances of child abuse as required by Section 11166 of the Penal Code.[37]

1037.4. As used in this article, "holder of the privilege" means:

(a) The victim when he or she has no guardian or conservator.

(b) A guardian or conservator of the victim when the victim has a guardian or conservator, unless the guardian or conservator is accused of perpetrating domestic violence against the victim.[104]

1037.5. A victim of domestic violence, whether or not a party to the action, has a privilege to refuse to disclose, and to prevent another from disclosing, a confidential communication between the victim and a domestic violence counselor in any proceeding specified in Section 901 if the privilege is claimed by any of the following persons:

(a) The holder of the privilege.

(b) A person who is authorized to claim the privilege by the holder of the privilege.

(c) The person who was the domestic violence counselor at the time of the confidential communication. However, that person may not claim the privilege if there is no holder of the privilege in existence or if he or she is otherwise instructed by a person authorized to permit disclosure.[105]

1037.6. The domestic violence counselor who received or made a communication subject to the privilege granted by this article shall claim the privilege whenever he or she is present when the communication is sought to be disclosed and he or she is authorized to claim the privilege under subdivision (c) of Section 1037.5.[37]

1037.7. As used in this article, "domestic violence" means "domestic violence" as defined in Section 6211 of the Family Code.[52]

1037.8. A domestic violence counselor shall inform a domestic violence victim of any applicable limitations on confidentiality of communications between the victim and the domestic violence counselor. This information may be given orally.[81]

Article 8.8: Human Trafficking Caseworker-Victim Privilege
Heading of Article 8.8 amended by Stats. 2006, Ch. 689, Sec. 9.

1038. (a) A trafficking victim, whether or not a party to the action, has a privilege to refuse to disclose, and to prevent another from disclosing, a confidential communication, whether made orally, in writing, or otherwise conveyed, between the victim and a human trafficking caseworker if the privilege is claimed by any of the following persons:

(1) The holder of the privilege.

(2) A person who is authorized to claim the privilege by the holder of the privilege.

(3) The person who was the human trafficking caseworker at the time of the confidential communication or is presently the human trafficking caseworker for the victim. However, that person may not claim the privilege if there is no holder of the privilege in existence or if the person is otherwise instructed by the court or by another person authorized to permit disclosure

(b) The human trafficking caseworker shall claim the privilege whenever the caseworker is present when the communication is sought to be disclosed and the caseworker is authorized to claim the privilege under this section.

(c) A human trafficking caseworker shall inform a trafficking victim of any applicable limitations on confidentiality of communications between the victim and the caseworker. This information may be given orally.[151]

1038.1. (a) The court may compel disclosure of information received by a human trafficking caseworker that constitutes relevant evidence of the facts and circumstances involving a crime allegedly perpetrated against the victim and that is the subject of a criminal proceeding, if the court determines that the probative value of the information outweighs the effect of disclosure of the information on the victim, the counseling relationship, and the counseling services.

(b) When a court rules on a claim of privilege under this article, it may require the person from whom disclosure is sought or the person authorized to claim the privilege, or both, to disclose the information in chambers out of the presence and hearing of all persons except the person authorized to claim the privilege and those other persons that the person authorized to claim the privilege consents to have present.

(c) If the judge determines that the information is privileged and shall not be disclosed, no person shall disclose, without the consent of a person authorized to permit disclosure, any information disclosed in the course of the proceedings in chambers. If the court determines that information shall be disclosed, the court shall so order and inform the defendant in the criminal action. If the court finds there is a reasonable likelihood that any information is subject to disclosure pursuant to the balancing test provided in this section, the procedure specified in paragraphs (1), (2), and (3) of Section 1035.4 shall be followed.[152]

1038.2. As used in this article, the following terms have the following meanings:

(a) "Confidential communication" means all information, including, but not limited to, written and oral communication, transmitted between the victim and the human trafficking caseworker in the course of their relationship and in confidence by a means which, so far as the victim is aware, discloses the information to no third persons other than those who are present to further the interests of the victim in the consultation or those to whom disclosures are reasonably necessary for the transmission of the information or an accomplishment of the purposes for which the human trafficking caseworker is consulted and made with the victim's knowledge and consent. "Confidential communication" includes all information regarding the facts and circumstances relating to all incidences of human trafficking, as well as all information about the children of the victim and the relationship of the victim to the human trafficker.

(b) "Holder of the privilege" means:

(1) The victim if the victim has no guardian or conservator.

(2) A guardian or conservator of the victim if the victim has a guardian or conservator.

(3) The personal representative of the victim if the victim is deceased.

(c) "Human trafficking caseworker" means a person working for a human trafficking victim service organization, whether financially compensated or not, for the purpose of rendering advice or assistance to victims of human trafficking, who meets the requirements of paragraph (1) or (2) and who also meets the requirements of paragraph (3), if applicable:

(1) Has an advanced degree or license, such as a master's degree in counseling, social work, or a related field and at least one year of experience in a caseworker role working directly with victims of human trafficking.

(2) Has at least 40 hours of training as specified in this paragraph and is supervised by an individual who qualifies as a human trafficking caseworker under paragraph (1). The training, supervised by a person qualified under paragraph (1), shall include, but need not be limited to, the following areas:

(A) History of human trafficking.

(B) Civil and criminal law relating to human trafficking.

(C) Systems of oppression.

(D) Peer counseling techniques.

(E) Resources available to victims of human trafficking.

(F) Crisis intervention and counseling techniques.

(G) Role playing.

(H) Intersections of human trafficking and other crimes.

(I) Client and system advocacy.

(J) Referral services.

(K) Connecting to local, regional, and national human trafficking coalitions.

(L) Explaining privileged communications.

(3) If the caseworker has been employed by a human trafficking service organization for a period of less than six months, that caseworker is supervised by another human trafficking

caseworker who has at least one year of experience working with human trafficking victims.

(d) "Human trafficking victim service organization" means a nongovernmental organization or entity that provides shelter, program, or other support services to victims of human trafficking and their children and that does all of the following:

(1) Employs staff that meet the requirements of a human trafficking caseworker as set forth in this section.

(2) Operates a telephone hotline, advertised to the public, for survivor crisis calls.

(3) Offers psychological support and peer counseling provided in accordance with this section.

(4) Makes staff available during normal business hours to assist victims of human trafficking who need shelter, programs, or other support services.

(e) "Victim" means a person who consults a human trafficking caseworker for the purpose of securing advice or assistance concerning a mental, physical, emotional, or other condition related to their experience as a victim of human trafficking.[158]

1038.3. Nothing in this article shall be construed as limiting any obligation to report instances of child abuse as required by Section 11166 of the Penal Code.[153]

Article 9: Official Information and Identity of Informer

Article 9 enacted by Stats. 1965, Ch. 299.

1040. (a) As used in this section, "official information" means information acquired in confidence by a public employee in the course of his or her duty and not open, or officially disclosed, to the public prior to the time the claim of privilege is made.

(b) A public entity has a privilege to refuse to disclose official information, and to prevent another from disclosing official information, if the privilege is claimed by a person authorized by the public entity to do so and either of the following apply:

(1) Disclosure is forbidden by an act of the Congress of the United States or a statute of this state.

(2) Disclosure of the information is against the public interest because there is a necessity for preserving the confidentiality of the information that outweighs the necessity for disclosure in the interest of justice; but no privilege may be claimed under this paragraph if any person authorized to do so has consented that the information be disclosed in the proceeding. In determining whether disclosure of the information is against the public interest, the interest of the public entity as a party in the outcome of the proceeding may not be considered.

(c) Notwithstanding any other law, the Employment Development Department shall disclose to law enforcement agencies, in accordance with subdivision (i) of Section 1095 of the Unemployment Insurance Code, information in its possession relating to any person if an arrest warrant has been issued for the person for commission of a felony.[123]

1041. (a) Except as provided in this section, a public entity has a privilege to refuse to disclose the identity of a person who has furnished information as provided in subdivision (b) purporting to disclose a violation of a law of the United States or of this state or of a public entity in this state, and to prevent another from disclosing the person's identity, if the privilege is claimed by a person authorized by the public entity to do so and either of the following apply:

(1) Disclosure is forbidden by an act of the Congress of the United States or a statute of this state.

(2) Disclosure of the identity of the informer is against the public interest because the necessity for preserving the confidentiality of his or her identity outweighs the necessity for disclosure in the interest of justice. The privilege shall not be claimed under this paragraph if a person authorized to do so has consented that the identity of the informer be disclosed in the proceeding. In determining whether disclosure of the identity of the informer is against the public interest, the interest of the public entity as a party in the outcome of the proceeding shall not be considered.

(b) The privilege described in this section applies only if the information is furnished in confidence by the informer to any of the following:

(1) A law enforcement officer.

(2) A representative of an administrative agency charged with the administration or enforcement of the law alleged to be violated.

(3) Any person for the purpose of transmittal to a person listed in paragraph (1) or (2). As used in this paragraph, "person" includes a volunteer or employee of a crime stopper organization.

(c) The privilege described in this section shall not be construed to prevent the informer from disclosing his or her identity.

(d) As used in this section, "crime stopper organization" means a private, nonprofit organization that accepts and expends donations used to reward persons who report to the organization information concerning alleged criminal activity, and forwards the information to the appropriate law enforcement agency.[118]

1042. (a) Except where disclosure is forbidden by an act of the Congress of the United States, if a claim of privilege under this article by the state or a public entity in this state is sustained in a criminal proceeding, the presiding officer shall make such order or finding of fact adverse to the public entity bringing the proceeding as is required by law upon any issue in the proceeding to which the privileged information is material.

(b) Notwithstanding subdivision (a), where a search is made pursuant to a warrant valid on its face, the public entity bringing a criminal proceeding is not required to reveal to the defendant official information or the identity of an informer in order to establish the legality of the search or the admissibility of any evidence obtained as a result of it.

(c) Notwithstanding subdivision (a), in any preliminary hearing, criminal trial, or other criminal proceeding, any otherwise admissible evidence of information communicated to a peace officer by a confidential informant, who is not a material witness to the guilt or innocence of the accused of the offense charged, is admissible on the issue of reasonable cause to make an arrest or search without requiring that the name or identity of the informant be disclosed if the judge or magistrate is satisfied, based upon evidence produced in open court, out of the presence of the jury, that such information was received from a reliable informant and in his discretion does not require such disclosure.

(d) When, in any such criminal proceeding, a party demands disclosure of the identity of the informant on the ground the informant is a material witness on the issue of guilt, the court shall conduct a hearing at which all parties may present evidence on the issue of disclosure. Such hearing shall be conducted outside the presence of the jury, if any. During the hearing, if the privilege provided for in Section 1041 is claimed by a person authorized to do so or if a person who is authorized to claim such privilege refuses to answer any question on the ground that the answer would tend to disclose the identity of the informant, the prosecuting attorney may request that the court hold an in camera hearing. If such a request is made, the court shall hold such a hearing outside the presence of the defendant and his counsel. At the in camera hearing, the prosecution may offer evidence which would tend to disclose or which discloses the identity of the informant to aid the court in its determination whether there is a reasonable possibility that nondisclosure might deprive the defendant of a fair trial. A reporter shall be present at the in camera hearing. Any transcription of the proceedings at the in camera hearing, as well as any physical evidence presented at the hearing, shall be ordered sealed by the court, and only a court may have access to its contents. The court shall not order disclosure, nor strike the testimony of the witness who invokes the privilege, nor dismiss the criminal proceeding, if the party offering the witness refuses to disclose the identity of the informant, unless, based upon the evidence presented at the hearing held in the presence of the defendant and his counsel and the evidence presented at the in camera hearing, the court concludes that there is a reasonable possibility that nondisclosure might deprive the defendant of a fair trial.[7]

1043. (a) In any case in which discovery or disclosure is sought of peace or custodial officer personnel records or records maintained pursuant to Section 832.5 of the Penal Code or information from those records, the party seeking the discovery or disclosure shall file a written motion with the appropriate court or administrative body upon written notice to the governmental agency that has custody and control of the records, as follows:

(1) In a civil action, the written notice shall be given at the times prescribed by subdivision (b) of Section 1005 of the Code of Civil Procedure.

(2) In a criminal action, the written notice shall be served and filed at least 10 court days before the hearing. All papers opposing a motion so noticed shall be filed with the court at least five court days, and all reply papers at least two court days, before the hearing. Proof of service of the notice shall be filed no later than five court days before the hearing.

(b) The motion shall include all of the following:

(1) Identification of the proceeding in which discovery or disclosure is sought, the party seeking discovery or disclosure, the peace or custodial officer whose records are sought, the governmental agency that has custody

and control of the records, and the time and place at which the motion for discovery or disclosure shall be heard.

(2) A description of the type of records or information sought.

(3) Affidavits showing good cause for the discovery or disclosure sought, setting forth the materiality thereof to the subject matter involved in the pending litigation and stating upon reasonable belief that the governmental agency identified has the records or information from the records.

(c) Upon receipt of a notice served pursuant to subdivision (a), the governmental agency shall immediately notify the individual whose records are sought.

(d) No hearing upon a motion for discovery or disclosure shall be held without full compliance with the notice provisions of this section except upon a showing by the moving party of good cause for noncompliance, or upon a waiver of the hearing by the governmental agency identified as having the records.[155]

1044. Nothing in this article shall be construed to affect the right of access to records of medical or psychological history where such access would otherwise be available under Section 996 or 1016.[21]

1045. (a) This article does not affect the right of access to records of complaints, or investigations of complaints, or discipline imposed as a result of those investigations, concerning an event or transaction in which the peace officer or custodial officer, as defined in Section 831.5 of the Penal Code, participated, or which the officer perceived, and pertaining to the manner in which the officer performed the officer's duties, provided that information is relevant to the subject matter involved in the pending litigation.

(b) In determining relevance, the court shall examine the information in chambers in conformity with Section 915, and shall exclude from disclosure both of the following:

(1) In any criminal proceeding the conclusions of any officer investigating a complaint filed pursuant to Section 832.5 of the Penal Code.

(2) Facts sought to be disclosed that are so remote as to make disclosure of little or no practical benefit.

(c) In determining relevance where the issue in litigation concerns the policies or pattern of conduct of the employing agency, the court shall consider whether the information sought may be obtained from other records maintained by the employing agency in the regular course of agency business which would not necessitate the disclosure of individual personnel records.

(d) Upon motion seasonably made by the governmental agency which has custody or control of the records to be examined or by the officer whose records are sought, and upon good cause showing the necessity thereof, the court may make any order which justice requires to protect the officer or agency from unnecessary annoyance, embarrassment or oppression.

(e) The court shall, in any case or proceeding permitting the disclosure or discovery of any peace or custodial officer records requested pursuant to Section 1043, order that the records disclosed or discovered may not be used for any purpose other than a court proceeding pursuant to applicable law.[160]

1046. In any case, otherwise authorized by law, in which the party seeking disclosure is alleging excessive force by a peace officer or custodial officer, as defined in Section 831.5 of the Penal Code, in connection with the arrest of that party, or for conduct alleged to have occurred within a jail facility, the motion shall include a copy of the police report setting forth the circumstances under which the party was stopped and arrested, or a copy of the crime report setting forth the circumstances under which the conduct is alleged to have occurred within a jail facility.[80]

1047. (a) Records of peace officers or custodial officers, as defined in Section 831.5 of the Penal Code, including supervisorial officers, who either were not present during the arrest or had no contact with the party seeking disclosure from the time of the arrest until the time of booking, or who were not present at the time the conduct at issue is alleged to have occurred within a jail facility, shall not be subject to disclosure.
(b) Notwithstanding subdivision (a), if a supervisorial officer whose records are being sought had direct oversight of a peace officer or a custodial officer, as defined in Section 831.5 of the Penal Code and issued command directives or had command influence over the circumstances at issue, the supervisorial officer's records shall be subject to disclosure pursuant to Section 1045 if the peace officer or custodial officer under supervision was present during the arrest, had contact with the party seeking disclosure from the time of the arrest until the time of booking, or was present at the time the conduct at issue is alleged to have occurred within a jail facility.[156]

Article 10: Political Vote
Article 10 enacted by Stats. 1965, Ch. 299.

1050. If he claims the privilege, a person has a privilege to refuse to disclose the tenor of his vote at a public election where the voting is by secret ballot unless he voted illegally or he previously made an unprivileged disclosure of the tenor of his vote.[1]

Article 11: Trade Secret
Article 11 enacted by Stats. 1965, Ch. 299.

1060. If he or his agent or employee claims the privilege, the owner of a trade secret has a privilege to refuse to disclose the secret, and to prevent another from disclosing it, if the allowance of the privilege will not tend to conceal fraud or otherwise work injustice.[1]

1061. (a) For purposes of this section, and Sections 1062 and 1063:
(1) "Trade secret" means "trade secret," as defined in subdivision (d) of Section 3426.1 of the Civil Code, or paragraph (9) of subdivision (a) of Section 499c of the Penal Code.
(2) "Article" means "article," as defined in paragraph (2) of subdivision (a) of Section 499c of the Penal Code.
(b) In addition to Section 1062, the following procedure shall apply whenever the owner of a trade secret wishes to assert his or her trade secret privilege, as provided in Section 1060, during a criminal proceeding:
(1) The owner of the trade secret shall file a motion for a protective order, or the people may file the motion on the

owner's behalf and with the owner's permission. The motion shall include an affidavit based upon personal knowledge listing the affiant's qualifications to give an opinion concerning the trade secret at issue, identifying, without revealing, the alleged trade secret and articles which disclose the secret, and presenting evidence that the secret qualifies as a trade secret under either subdivision (d) of Section 3426.1 of the Civil Code or paragraph (9) of subdivision (a) of Section 499c of the Penal Code. The motion and affidavit shall be served on all parties in the proceeding.

(2) Any party in the proceeding may oppose the request for the protective order by submitting affidavits based upon the affiant's personal knowledge. The affidavits shall be filed under seal, but shall be provided to the owner of the trade secret and to all parties in the proceeding. Neither the owner of the trade secret nor any party in the proceeding may disclose the affidavit to persons other than to counsel of record without prior court approval.

(3) The movant shall, by a preponderance of the evidence, show that the issuance of a protective order is proper. The court may rule on the request without holding an evidentiary hearing. However, in its discretion, the court may choose to hold an in camera evidentiary hearing concerning disputed articles with only the owner of the trade secret, the people's representative, the defendant, and defendant's counsel present. If the court holds such a hearing, the parties' right to examine witnesses shall not be used to obtain discovery, but shall be directed solely toward the question of whether the alleged trade secret qualifies for protection.

(4) If the court finds that a trade secret may be disclosed during any criminal proceeding unless a protective order is issued and that the issuance of a protective order would not conceal a fraud or work an injustice, the court shall issue a protective order limiting the use and dissemination of the trade secret, including, but not limited to, articles disclosing that secret. The protective order may, in the court's discretion, include the following provisions:

(A) That the trade secret may be disseminated only to counsel for the parties, including their associate attorneys, paralegals, and investigators, and to law enforcement officials or clerical officials.

(B) That the defendant may view the secret only in the presence of his or her counsel, or if not in the presence of his or her counsel, at counsel's offices.

(C) That any party seeking to show the trade secret, or articles containing the trade secret, to any person not designated by the protective order shall first obtain court approval to do so:

(i) The court may require that the person receiving the trade secret do so only in the presence of counsel for the party requesting approval.

(ii) The court may require the person receiving the trade secret to sign a copy of the protective order and to agree to be bound by its terms. The order may include a provision recognizing the owner of the trade secret to be a third-party beneficiary of that agreement.

(iii) The court may require a party

seeking disclosure to an expert to provide that expert's name, employment history, and any other relevant information to the court for examination. The court shall accept that information under seal, and the information shall not be disclosed by any court except upon termination of the action and upon a showing of good cause to believe the secret has been disseminated by a court-approved expert. The court shall evaluate the expert and determine whether the expert poses a discernible risk of disclosure. The court shall withhold approval if the expert's economic interests place the expert in a competitive position with the victim, unless no other experts are available. The court may interview the expert in camera in aid of its ruling. If the court rejects the expert, it shall state its reasons for doing so on the record and a transcript of those reasons shall be prepared and sealed.

(D) That no articles disclosing the trade secret shall be filed or otherwise made a part of the court record available to the public without approval of the court and prior notice to the owner of the secret. The owner of the secret may give either party permission to accept the notice on the owner's behalf.

(E) Other orders as the court deems necessary to protect the integrity of the trade secret.

(c) A ruling granting or denying a motion for a protective order filed pursuant to subdivision (b) shall not be construed as a determination that the alleged trade secret is or is not a trade secret as defined by subdivision (d) of Section 3426.1 of the Civil Code or paragraph (9) of subdivision (a) of Section 499c of the Penal Code. Such a ruling shall not have any effect on any civil litigation.

(d) This section shall have prospective effect only and shall not operate to invalidate previously entered protective orders.[83]

1062. (a) Notwithstanding any other provision of law, in a criminal case, the court, upon motion of the owner of a trade secret, or upon motion by the People with the consent of the owner, may exclude the public from any portion of a criminal proceeding where the proponent of closure has demonstrated a substantial probability that the trade secret would otherwise be disclosed to the public during that proceeding and a substantial probability that the disclosure would cause serious harm to the owner of the secret, and where the court finds that there is no overriding public interest in an open proceeding. No evidence, however, shall be excluded during a criminal proceeding pursuant to this section if it would conceal a fraud, work an injustice, or deprive the People or the defendant of a fair trial.

(b) The motion made pursuant to subdivision (a) shall identify, without revealing, the trade secrets which would otherwise be disclosed to the public. A showing made pursuant to subdivision (a) shall be made during an in camera hearing with only the owner of the trade secret, the People's representative, the defendant, and defendant's counsel present. A court reporter shall be present during the hearing. Any transcription of the proceedings at the in camera hearing, as well as any articles presented at that hearing, shall be ordered sealed by the court and only a court may allow access to its contents upon a showing of good cause. The court, in ruling upon the motion made pursuant to subdivision (a), may consider testimony presented or affidavits filed in any proceeding held in that action.

(c) If, after the in camera hearing described in subdivision (b), the court determines that exclusion of trade secret information from the public is appropriate, the court shall close only that portion of the criminal proceeding necessary to prevent disclosure of the trade secret. Before granting the motion, however, the court shall find and state for the record that the moving party has met its burden pursuant to subdivision (b), and that the closure of that portion of the proceeding will not deprive the People or the defendant of a fair trial.

(d) The owner of the trade secret, the People, or the defendant may seek relief from a ruling denying or granting closure by petitioning a higher court for extraordinary relief.

(e) Whenever the court closes a portion of a criminal proceeding pursuant to this section, a transcript of that closed proceeding shall be made available to the public as soon as practicable. The court shall redact any information qualifying as a trade secret before making that transcript available.

(f) The court, subject to Section 867 of the Penal Code, may allow witnesses who are bound by a protective order entered in the criminal proceeding protecting trade secrets, pursaunt to Section 1061, to remain within the courtroom during the closed portion of the proceeding.[47]

1063. The following provisions shall govern requests to seal articles which are protected by a protective order entered pursuant to Evidence Code Section 1060 or 1061:

(a) The People shall request sealing of articles reasonably expected to be filed or admitted into evidence as follows:

(1) No less than 10 court days before trial, and no less than five court days before any other criminal proceeding, the People shall file with the court a list of all articles which the People reasonably expect to file with the court, or admit into evidence, under seal at that proceeding. That list shall be available to the public. The People may be relieved from providing timely notice upon showing that exigent circumstances prevent that notice.

(2) The court shall not allow the listed articles to be filed, admitted into evidence, or in any way made a part of the court record otherwise open to the public before holding a hearing to consider any objections to the People's request to seal the articles. The court at that hearing shall allow those objecting to the sealing to state their objections.

(3) After hearing any objections to sealing, the court shall conduct an in camera hearing with only the owner of the trade secret contained within those articles, the People's representative, defendant, and defendant's counsel present. The court shall review the articles sought to be sealed, evaluate objections to sealing, and determine whether the People have satisfied the constitutional standards governing public access to articles which are part of the judicial record. The court may consider testimony presented or affidavits filed in any proceeding held in that action. The People, defendant, and the owner of

the trade secret may file affidavits based on the affiant's personal knowledge to be considered at that hearing. Those affidavits are to be sealed and not released to the public, but shall be made available to the parties. The court may rule on the request to seal without taking testimony. If the court takes testimony, examination of witnesses shall not be used to obtain discovery, but shall be directed solely toward whether sealing is appropriate.

(4) If the court finds that the movant has satisfied appropriate constitutional standards with respect to sealing particular articles, the court shall seal those articles if and when they are filed, admitted into evidence, or in any way made a part of the court record otherwise open to the public. The articles shall not be unsealed absent an order of a court upon a showing of good cause. Failure to examine the court file for notice of a request to seal shall not constitute good cause to consider objections to sealing.

(b) The following procedure shall apply to other articles made a part of the court record:

(1) Where any articles protected by a protective order entered pursuant to Section 1060 or 1061 are filed, admitted into evidence, or in any way made a part of the court record in such a way as to be otherwise open to the public, the People, a defendant, or the owner of a trade secret contained within those articles may request the court to seal those articles.

(2) The request to seal shall be made by noticed motion filed with the court. It may also be made orally in court at the time the articles are made a part of the court record. Where the request is made orally, the movant must file within 24 hours a written description of that request, including a list of the articles which are the subject of that request. These motions and lists shall be available to the public.

(3) The court shall promptly conduct hearings as provided in paragraphs (2), (3), and (4) of subdivision (a). The court shall, pending the hearings, seal those articles which are the subject of the request. Where a request to seal is made orally, the court may conduct hearings at the time the articles are made a part of the court record, but shall reconsider its ruling in light of additional objections made by objectors within two court days after the written record of the request to seal is made available to the public.

(4) Any articles sealed pursuant to these hearings shall not be unsealed absent an order of a court upon a showing of good cause. Failure to examine the court file for notice of a request to seal shall not constitute good cause to consider objections to sealing.[48]

Chapter 5: Immunity of Newsman From Citation for Contempt

Chapter 5 enacted by Stats. 1965, Ch. 299.

1070. (a) A publisher, editor, reporter, or other person connected with or employed upon a newspaper, magazine, or other periodical publication, or by a press association or wire service, or any person who has been so connected or employed, cannot be adjudged in contempt by a judicial, legislative, administrative body, or any other body having the power to issue subpoenas, for refusing to disclose, in any proceeding as defined in Section 901, the source of any information procured while so connected or employed for publication in a newspaper, magazine or other periodical publication, or for refusing to disclose any unpublished information obtained or prepared in gathering, receiving or processing of information for communication to the public.

(b) Nor can a radio or television news reporter or other person connected with or employed by a radio or television station, or any person who has been so connected or employed, be so adjudged in contempt for refusing to disclose the source of any information procured while so connected or employed for news or news commentary purposes on radio or television, or for refusing to disclose any unpublished information obtained or prepared in gathering, receiving or processing of information for communication to the public.

(c) As used in this section, "unpublished information" includes information not disseminated to the public by the person from whom disclosure is sought, whether or not related information has been disseminated and includes, but is not limited to, all notes, outtakes, photographs, tapes or other data of whatever sort not itself disseminated to the public through a medium of communication, whether or not published information based upon or related to such material has been disseminated.[13]

DIVISION 9: EVIDENCE AFFECTED OR EXCLUDED BY EXTRINSIC POLICIES

DIVISION 9 ENACTED BY STATS. 1965, CH. 299.
SECTION 1100 - 1162

Chapter 1: Evidence of Character, Habit, or Custom

Chapter 1 enacted by Stats. 1965, Ch. 299.

1100. Except as otherwise provided by statute, any otherwise admissible evidence (including evidence in the form of an opinion, evidence of reputation, and evidence of specific instances of such person's conduct) is admissible to prove a person's character or a trait of his character.[1]

1101. (a) Except as provided in this section and in Sections 1102, 1103, 1108, and 1109, evidence of a person's character or a trait of his or her character (whether in the form of an opinion, evidence of reputation, or evidence of specific instances of his or her conduct) is inadmissible when offered to prove his or her conduct on a specified occasion.
(b) Nothing in this section prohibits the admission of evidence that a person committed a crime, civil wrong, or other act when relevant to prove some fact (such as motive, opportunity, intent, preparation, plan, knowledge, identity, absence of mistake or accident, or whether a defendant in a prosecution for an unlawful sexual act or attempted unlawful sexual act did not reasonably and in good faith believe that the victim consented) other than his or her disposition to commit such an act.
(c) Nothing in this section affects the admissibility of evidence offered to support or attack the credibility of a witness.[63]

1102. In a criminal action, evidence of the defendant's character or a trait of his character in the form of an opinion or evidence of his reputation is not made inadmissible by Section 1101 if such evidence is:
(a) Offered by the defendant to prove his conduct in conformity with such character or trait of character.
(b) Offered by the prosecution to rebut evidence adduced by the defendant under subdivision (a).[1]

1103. (a) In a criminal action, evidence of the character or a trait of character (in the form of an opinion, evidence of reputation, or evidence of specific instances of conduct) of the victim of the crime for which the defendant is being prosecuted is not made inadmissible by Section 1101 if the evidence is:
(1) Offered by the defendant to prove conduct of the victim in conformity with the character or trait of character.
(2) Offered by the prosecution to rebut evidence adduced by the defendant under paragraph (1).
(b) In a criminal action, evidence of the defendant's character for violence or trait of character for violence (in the form of an opinion, evidence of reputation, or evidence of specific instances of conduct) is not made inadmissible by Section 1101 if the evidence is offered by the prosecution to

prove conduct of the defendant in conformity with the character or trait of character and is offered after evidence that the victim had a character for violence or a trait of character tending to show violence has been adduced by the defendant under paragraph (1) of subdivision (a).

(c) (1) Notwithstanding any other provision of this code to the contrary, and except as provided in this subdivision, in any prosecution under Section 261 or 264.1 of the Penal Code, or under Section 286, 287, or 289 of, or former Section 262 or 288a of, the Penal Code, or for assault with intent to commit, attempt to commit, or conspiracy to commit a crime defined in any of those sections, except where the crime is alleged to have occurred in a local detention facility, as defined in Section 6031.4, or in a state prison, as defined in Section 4504, opinion evidence, reputation evidence, and evidence of specific instances of the complaining witness' sexual conduct, or any of that evidence, is not admissible by the defendant in order to prove consent by the complaining witness.

(2) Notwithstanding paragraph (3), evidence of the manner in which the victim was dressed at the time of the commission of the offense is not admissible when offered by either party on the issue of consent in any prosecution for an offense specified in paragraph (1). For the purposes of this paragraph, "manner of dress" does not include the condition of the victim's clothing before, during, or after the commission of the offense.

(3) Paragraph (1) does not apply to evidence of the complaining witness' sexual conduct with the defendant.

(4) If the prosecutor introduces evidence, including testimony of a witness, or the complaining witness as a witness gives testimony, and that evidence or testimony relates to the complaining witness' sexual conduct, the defendant may cross-examine the witness who gives the testimony and offer relevant evidence limited specifically to the rebuttal of the evidence introduced by the prosecutor or given by the complaining witness.

(5) This subdivision does not make inadmissible any evidence offered to attack the credibility of the complaining witness as provided in Section 782.

(6) As used in this subdivision, "complaining witness" means the alleged victim of the crime charged, the prosecution of which is subject to this subdivision.[167]

1104. Except as provided in Sections 1102 and 1103, evidence of a trait of a person's character with respect to care or skill is inadmissible to prove the quality of his conduct on a specified occasion.[1]

1105. Any otherwise admissible evidence of habit or custom is admissible to prove conduct on a specified occasion in conformity with the habit or custom.[1]

1106. (a) In any civil action alleging conduct which constitutes sexual harassment, sexual assault, or sexual battery, opinion evidence, reputation evidence, and evidence of specific instances of the plaintiff's sexual conduct, or any of that evidence, is not admissible by the defendant in order to:

(1) Prove consent by the plaintiff.

(2) Prove absence of injury suffered

by the plaintiff, unless the injury alleged by the plaintiff is in the nature of loss of consortium.
(3) Attack the credibility of the plaintiff's testimony on consent or the absence of injury suffered by the plaintiff.
(b) Subdivision (a) does not apply to evidence of the plaintiff's sexual conduct with the alleged perpetrator.
(c) Notwithstanding subdivision (b), in any civil action brought pursuant to Section 1708.5 of the Civil Code involving a minor and an adult as described in Section 1708.5.5 of the Civil Code, evidence of the plaintiff minor's sexual conduct with the defendant adult shall not be admissible to prove consent by the plaintiff or the absence of injury to the plaintiff.
(d) If the plaintiff introduces evidence, including testimony of a witness, or the plaintiff as a witness gives testimony, and the evidence or testimony relates to the plaintiff's sexual conduct, the defendant may cross-examine the witness who gives the testimony and offer relevant evidence limited specifically to the rebuttal of the evidence introduced by the plaintiff or given by the plaintiff.
(e) This section shall not be construed to make inadmissible any evidence offered to attack the credibility of the plaintiff's testimony as to something other than consent or absence of injury as provided in Section 783.[175]

1107. (a) In a criminal action, expert testimony is admissible by either the prosecution or the defense regarding intimate partner battering and its effects, including the nature and effect of physical, emotional, or mental abuse on the beliefs, perceptions, or behavior of victims of domestic violence, except when offered against a criminal defendant to prove the occurrence of the act or acts of abuse which form the basis of the criminal charge.
(b) The foundation shall be sufficient for admission of this expert testimony if the proponent of the evidence establishes its relevancy and the proper qualifications of the expert witness. Expert opinion testimony on intimate partner battering and its effects shall not be considered a new scientific technique whose reliability is unproven.
(c) For purposes of this section, "abuse" is defined in Section 6203 of the Family Code, and "domestic violence" is defined in Section 6211 of the Family Code and may include acts defined in Section 242, subdivision (e) of Section 243, Section 261, 273.5, 273.6, 422, or 653m of, or former Section 262 of, the Penal Code.
(d) This section is intended as a rule of evidence only and no substantive change affecting the Penal Code is intended.
(e) This section shall be known, and may be cited, as the Expert Witness Testimony on Intimate Partner Battering and Its Effects Section of the Evidence Code.
(f) The changes in this section that become effective on January 1, 2005, are not intended to impact any existing decisional law regarding this section, and that decisional law should apply equally to this section as it refers to "intimate partner battering and its effects" in place of "battered women's syndrome."[168]

1107.5. (a) In a criminal action, expert testimony is admissible by either the prosecution or the defense regarding the effects of human trafficking on human trafficking victims, including the nature and effect of physical, emotional, or mental abuse on the beliefs, perceptions, or behavior of human trafficking victims.

(b) The foundation shall be sufficient for admission of this expert testimony if the proponent of the evidence establishes its relevancy and the proper qualifications of the expert witness.

(c) For purposes of this section, "human trafficking victim" is defined as a victim of an offense described in Section 236.1 of the Penal Code.

(d) This section is intended as a rule of evidence only and no substantive change affecting the Penal Code is intended.[136]

1108. (a) In a criminal action in which the defendant is accused of a sexual offense, evidence of the defendant's commission of another sexual offense or offenses is not made inadmissible by Section 1101, if the evidence is not inadmissible pursuant to Section 352.

(b) In an action in which evidence is to be offered under this section, the people shall disclose the evidence to the defendant, including statements of witnesses or a summary of the substance of any testimony that is expected to be offered in compliance with the requirements of Section 1054.7 of the Penal Code.

(c) This section does not limit the admission or consideration of evidence under any other section of this code.

(d) As used in this section, the following definitions shall apply:

(1) "Sexual offense" means a crime under the law of a state or of the United States that involved any of the following:

(A) Any conduct proscribed by subdivision (b) or (c) of Section 236.1, Section 243.4, 261, 261.5, 262, 264.1, 266c, 269, 286, 287, 288, 288.2, 288.5, or 289, or subdivision (b), (c), or (d) of Section 311.2 or Section 311.3, 311.4, 311.10, 311.11, 314, or 647.6 of, or former Section 288a of, the Penal Code.

(B) Any conduct proscribed by Section 220 of the Penal Code, except assault with intent to commit mayhem.

(C) Contact, without consent, between any part of the defendant's body or an object and the genitals or anus of another person.

(D) Contact, without consent, between the genitals or anus of the defendant and any part of another person's body.

(E) Deriving sexual pleasure or gratification from the infliction of death, bodily injury, or physical pain on another person.

(F) An attempt or conspiracy to engage in conduct described in this paragraph.

(2) "Consent" shall have the same meaning as provided in Section 261.6 of the Penal Code, except that it does not include consent which is legally ineffective because of the age, mental disorder, or developmental or physical disability of the victim.[147]

1109. (a) (1) Except as provided in subdivision (e) or (f), in a criminal action in which the defendant is accused of an offense involving domestic violence, evidence of the defendant's commission of other domestic violence is not made inadmissible by Section 1101 if the evidence is not inadmissible pursuant to Section 352.

(2) Except as provided in subdivision (e) or (f), in a criminal action in which the defendant is accused of an offense involving abuse of an elder or dependent person, evidence of the defendant's commission of other abuse of an elder or dependent person is not made inadmissible by Section 1101 if the evidence is not inadmissible pursuant to Section 352.

(3) Except as provided in subdivision (e) or (f) and subject to a hearing conducted pursuant to Section 352, which shall include consideration of any corroboration and remoteness in time, in a criminal action in which the defendant is accused of an offense involving child abuse, evidence of the defendant's commission of child abuse is not made inadmissible by Section 1101 if the evidence is not inadmissible pursuant to Section 352. Nothing in this paragraph prohibits or limits the admission of evidence pursuant to subdivision (b) of Section 1101.

(b) In an action in which evidence is to be offered under this section, the people shall disclose the evidence to the defendant, including statements of witnesses or a summary of the substance of any testimony that is expected to be offered, in compliance with the provisions of Section 1054.7 of the Penal Code.

(c) This section shall not be construed to limit or preclude the admission or consideration of evidence under any other statute or case law.

(d) As used in this section:

(1) "Abuse of an elder or dependent person" means physical or sexual abuse, neglect, financial abuse, abandonment, isolation, abduction, or other treatment that results in physical harm, pain, or mental suffering, the deprivation of care by a caregiver, or other deprivation by a custodian or provider of goods or services that are necessary to avoid physical harm or mental suffering.

(2) "Child abuse" means an act proscribed by Section 273d of the Penal Code.

(3) "Domestic violence" has the meaning set forth in Section 13700 of the Penal Code. Subject to a hearing conducted pursuant to Section 352, which shall include consideration of any corroboration and remoteness in time, "domestic violence" has the further meaning as set forth in Section 6211 of the Family Code, if the act occurred no more than five years before the charged offense.

(e) Evidence of acts occurring more than 10 years before the charged offense is inadmissible under this section, unless the court determines that the admission of this evidence is in the interest of justice.

(f) Evidence of the findings and determinations of administrative agencies regulating the conduct of health facilities licensed under Section 1250 of the Health and Safety Code is inadmissible under this section.[98]

Chapter 2: Mediation

Chapter 2 added by Stats. 1997, Ch. 772, Sec. 3.

1115. For purposes of this chapter:

(a) "Mediation" means a process in which a neutral person or persons facilitate communication between the

disputants to assist them in reaching a mutually acceptable agreement.
(b) "Mediator" means a neutral person who conducts a mediation. "Mediator" includes any person designated by a mediator either to assist in the mediation or to communicate with the participants in preparation for a mediation.
(c) "Mediation consultation" means a communication between a person and a mediator for the purpose of initiating, considering, or reconvening a mediation or retaining the mediator.[67]

1116. (a) Nothing in this chapter expands or limits a court's authority to order participation in a dispute resolution proceeding. Nothing in this chapter authorizes or affects the enforceability of a contract clause in which parties agree to the use of mediation.
(b) Nothing in this chapter makes admissible evidence that is inadmissible under Section 1152 or any other statute.[67]

1117. (a) Except as provided in subdivision (b), this chapter applies to a mediation as defined in Section 1115.
(b) This chapter does not apply to either of the following:
(1) A proceeding under Part 1 (commencing with Section 1800) of Division 5 of the Family Code or Chapter 11 (commencing with Section 3160) of Part 2 of Division 8 of the Family Code.
(2) A settlement conference pursuant to Rule 3.1380 of the California Rules of Court.[102]

1118. An oral agreement "in accordance with Section 1118" means an oral agreement that satisfies all of the following conditions:
(a) The oral agreement is recorded by a court reporter or reliable means of audio recording.
(b) The terms of the oral agreement are recited on the record in the presence of the parties and the mediator, and the parties express on the record that they agree to the terms recited.
(c) The parties to the oral agreement expressly state on the record that the agreement is enforceable or binding, or words to that effect.
(d) The recording is reduced to writing and the writing is signed by the parties within 72 hours after it is recorded.[109]

1119. Except as otherwise provided in this chapter:
(a) No evidence of anything said or any admission made for the purpose of, in the course of, or pursuant to, a mediation or a mediation consultation is admissible or subject to discovery, and disclosure of the evidence shall not be compelled, in any arbitration, administrative adjudication, civil action, or other noncriminal proceeding in which, pursuant to law, testimony can be compelled to be given.
(b) No writing, as defined in Section 250, that is prepared for the purpose of, in the course of, or pursuant to, a mediation or a mediation consultation, is admissible or subject to discovery, and disclosure of the writing shall not be compelled, in any arbitration, administrative adjudication, civil action, or other noncriminal proceeding in which, pursuant to law, testimony can be compelled to be given.
(c) All communications, negotiations, or settlement discussions by and between participants in the course of a mediation or a mediation consultation shall remain confidential.[67]

1120. (a) Evidence otherwise admissible or subject to discovery outside of a mediation or a mediation consultation shall not be or become inadmissible or protected from disclosure solely by reason of its introduction or use in a mediation or a mediation consultation.
(b) This chapter does not limit any of the following:
(1) The admissibility of an agreement to mediate a dispute.
(2) The effect of an agreement not to take a default or an agreement to extend the time within which to act or refrain from acting in a pending civil action.
(3) Disclosure of the mere fact that a mediator has served, is serving, will serve, or was contacted about serving as a mediator in a dispute.
(4) The admissibility of declarations of disclosure required by Sections 2104 and 2105 of the Family Code, even if prepared for the purpose of, in the course of, or pursuant to, a mediation or a mediation consultation.[134]

1121. Neither a mediator nor anyone else may submit to a court or other adjudicative body, and a court or other adjudicative body may not consider, any report, assessment, evaluation, recommendation, or finding of any kind by the mediator concerning a mediation conducted by the mediator, other than a report that is mandated by court rule or other law and that states only whether an agreement was reached, unless all parties to the mediation expressly agree otherwise in writing, or orally in accordance with Section 1118.[67]

1122. (a) A communication or a writing, as defined in Section 250, that is made or prepared for the purpose of, or in the course of, or pursuant to, a mediation or a mediation consultation, is not made inadmissible, or protected from disclosure, by provisions of this chapter if any of the following conditions are satisfied:
(1) All persons who conduct or otherwise participate in the mediation expressly agree in writing, or orally in accordance with Section 1118, to disclosure of the communication, document, or writing.
(2) The communication, document, or writing was prepared by or on behalf of fewer than all the mediation participants, those participants expressly agree in writing, or orally in accordance with Section 1118, to its disclosure, and the communication, document, or writing does not disclose anything said or done or any admission made in the course of the mediation.
(3) The communication, document, or writing is related to an attorney's compliance with the requirements described in Section 1129 and does not disclose anything said or done or any admission made in the course of the mediation, in which case the communication, document, or writing may be used in an attorney disciplinary proceeding to determine whether the attorney has complied with Section 1129.
(b) For purposes of subdivision (a), if the neutral person who conducts a mediation expressly agrees to disclosure, that agreement also binds any other person described in subdivision (b) of Section 1115.[144]

1123. A written settlement agreement prepared in the course of, or pursuant to, a mediation, is not made inadmissible, or protected from disclosure, by provisions of this chapter if the agreement is signed by the settling parties and any of the following conditions are satisfied:

(a) The agreement provides that it is admissible or subject to disclosure, or words to that effect.

(b) The agreement provides that it is enforceable or binding or words to that effect.

(c) All parties to the agreement expressly agree in writing, or orally in accordance with Section 1118, to its disclosure.

(d) The agreement is used to show fraud, duress, or illegality that is relevant to an issue in dispute.[67]

1124. An oral agreement made in the course of, or pursuant to, a mediation is not made inadmissible, or protected from disclosure, by the provisions of this chapter if any of the following conditions are satisfied:

(a) The agreement is in accordance with Section 1118.

(b) The agreement is in accordance with subdivisions (a), (b), and (d) of Section 1118, and all parties to the agreement expressly agree, in writing or orally in accordance with Section 1118, to disclosure of the agreement.

(c) The agreement is in accordance with subdivisions (a), (b), and (d) of Section 1118, and the agreement is used to show fraud, duress, or illegality that is relevant to an issue in dispute.[67]

1125. (a) For purposes of confidentiality under this chapter, a mediation ends when any one of the following conditions is satisfied:

(1) The parties execute a written settlement agreement that fully resolves the dispute.

(2) An oral agreement that fully resolves the dispute is reached in accordance with Section 1118.

(3) The mediator provides the mediation participants with a writing signed by the mediator that states that the mediation is terminated, or words to that effect, which shall be consistent with Section 1121.

(4) A party provides the mediator and the other mediation participants with a writing stating that the mediation is terminated, or words to that effect, which shall be consistent with Section 1121. In a mediation involving more than two parties, the mediation may continue as to the remaining parties or be terminated in accordance with this section.

(5) For 10 calendar days, there is no communication between the mediator and any of the parties to the mediation relating to the dispute. The mediator and the parties may shorten or extend this time by agreement.

(b) For purposes of confidentiality under this chapter, if a mediation partially resolves a dispute, mediation ends when either of the following conditions is satisfied:

(1) The parties execute a written settlement agreement that partially resolves the dispute.

(2) An oral agreement that partially resolves the dispute is reached in accordance with Section 1118.

(c) This section does not preclude a party from ending a mediation without reaching an agreement. This section does not otherwise affect the extent to which a party may terminate a mediation.[67]

1126. Anything said, any admission made, or any writing that is inadmissible, protected from disclosure, and confidential under this chapter before a mediation ends, shall remain inadmissible, protected from disclosure, and confidential to the same extent after the mediation ends.[67]

1127. If a person subpoenas or otherwise seeks to compel a mediator to testify or produce a writing, as defined in Section 250, and the court or other adjudicative body determines that the testimony or writing is inadmissible under this chapter, or protected from disclosure under this chapter, the court or adjudicative body making the determination shall award reasonable attorney's fees and costs to the mediator against the person seeking the testimony or writing.[67]

1128. Any reference to a mediation during any subsequent trial is an irregularity in the proceedings of the trial for the purposes of Section 657 of the Code of Civil Procedure. Any reference to a mediation during any other subsequent noncriminal proceeding is grounds for vacating or modifying the decision in that proceeding, in whole or in part, and granting a new or further hearing on all or part of the issues, if the reference materially affected the substantial rights of the party requesting relief.[67]

1129. (a) Except in the case of a class or representative action, an attorney representing a client participating in a mediation or a mediation consultation shall, as soon as reasonably possible before the client agrees to participate in the mediation or mediation consultation, provide that client with a printed disclosure containing the confidentiality restrictions described in Section 1119 and obtain a printed acknowledgment signed by that client stating that he or she has read and understands the confidentiality restrictions.

(b) An attorney who is retained after an individual agrees to participate in the mediation or mediation consultation shall, as soon as reasonably possible after being retained, comply with the printed disclosure and acknowledgment requirements described in subdivision (a).

(c) The printed disclosure required by subdivision (a) shall:

(1) Be printed in the preferred language of the client in at least 12-point font.

(2) Be printed on a single page that is not attached to any other document provided to the client.

(3) Include the names of the attorney and the client and be signed and dated by the attorney and the client.

(d) If the requirements in subdivision (c) are met, the following disclosure shall be deemed to comply with the requirements of subdivision (a):

Mediation Disclosure Notification and Acknowledgment

To promote communication in mediation, California law generally makes mediation a confidential process. California's mediation confidentiality laws are laid out in Sections 703.5 and 1115 to 1129, inclusive, of the Evidence Code. Those laws establish the confidentiality of mediation and limit the disclosure, admissibility, and a court's consideration of communications, writings, and conduct in connection with a mediation. In general, those laws mean the following:

• All communications, negotiations, or settlement offers in the course of a mediation must remain confidential.

• Statements made and writings prepared in connection with a mediation are not admissible or subject to discovery or compelled disclosure in noncriminal proceedings.

• A mediator's report, opinion, recommendation, or finding about what occurred in a mediation may not be submitted to or considered by a court or another adjudicative body.

• A mediator cannot testify in any subsequent civil proceeding about any communication or conduct occurring at, or in connection with, a mediation.

This means that all communications between you and your attorney made in preparation for a mediation, or during a mediation, are confidential and cannot be disclosed or used (except in extremely limited circumstances), even if you later decide to sue your attorney for malpractice because of something that happens during the mediation.

I, ______________ [Name of Client], understand that, unless all participants agree otherwise, no oral or written communication made during a mediation, or in preparation for a mediation, including communications between me and my attorney, can be used as evidence in any subsequent noncriminal legal action including an action against my attorney for malpractice or an ethical violation.

NOTE: This disclosure and signed acknowledgment does not limit your attorney's potential liability to you for professional malpractice, or prevent you from (1) reporting any professional misconduct by your attorney to the State Bar of California or (2) cooperating with any disciplinary investigation or criminal prosecution of your attorney.

[Name of Client] [Date signed]

[Name of Attorney] [Date signed]

(e) Failure of an attorney to comply with this section is not a basis to set aside an agreement prepared in the course of, or pursuant to, a mediation.[145]

Chapter 3: Other Evidence Affected or Excluded by Extrinsic Policies

Heading of Chapter 3 renumbered from Chapter 2 by Stats. 1997, Ch. 772, Sec. 4.

1150. (a) Upon an inquiry as to the validity of a verdict, any otherwise admissible evidence may be received as to statements made, or conduct, conditions, or events occurring, either within or without the jury room, of such a character as is likely to have influenced the verdict improperly. No evidence is admissible to show the effect of such statement, conduct, condition, or event upon a juror either in influencing him to assent to or dissent from the verdict or concerning the mental processes by which it was determined.

(b) Nothing in this code affects the law relating to the competence of a juror to give evidence to impeach or support a verdict.[1]

1151. When, after the occurrence of an event, remedial or precautionary measures are taken, which, if taken previously, would have tended to make the event less likely to occur, evidence of such subsequent measures is inadmissible to prove negligence or culpable conduct in connection with the event.[1]

1152. (a) Evidence that a person has, in compromise or from humanitarian motives, furnished or offered or promised to furnish money or any other thing, act, or service to another who has sustained or will sustain or claims that he or she has sustained or will sustain loss or damage, as well as any conduct or statements made in negotiation thereof, is inadmissible to prove his or her liability for the loss or damage or any part of it.

(b) In the event that evidence of an offer to compromise is admitted in an action for breach of the covenant of good faith and fair dealing or violation of subdivision (h) of Section 790.03 of the Insurance Code, then at the request of the party against whom the evidence is admitted, or at the request of the party who made the offer to compromise that was admitted, evidence relating to any other offer or counteroffer to compromise the same or substantially the same claimed loss or damage shall also be admissible for the same purpose as the initial evidence regarding settlement. Other than as may be admitted in an action for breach of the covenant of good faith and fair dealing or violation of subdivision (h) of Section 790.03 of the Insurance Code, evidence of settlement offers shall not be admitted in a motion for a new trial, in any proceeding involving an additur or remittitur, or on appeal.

(c) This section does not affect the admissibility of evidence of any of the following:

(1) Partial satisfaction of an asserted claim or demand without questioning its validity when such evidence is offered to prove the validity of the claim.

(2) A debtor's payment or promise to pay all or a part of his or her preexist-

ing debt when such evidence is offered to prove the creation of a new duty on his or her part or a revival of his or her preexisting duty.[39]

1153. Evidence of a plea of guilty, later withdrawn, or of an offer to plead guilty to the crime charged or to any other crime, made by the defendant in a criminal action is inadmissible in any action or in any proceeding of any nature, including proceedings before agencies, commissions, boards, and tribunals.[1]

1153.5. Evidence of an offer for civil resolution of a criminal matter pursuant to the provisions of Section 33 of the Code of Civil Procedure, or admissions made in the course of or negotiations for the offer shall not be admissible in any action.[28]

1154. Evidence that a person has accepted or offered or promised to accept a sum of money or any other thing, act, or service in satisfaction of a claim, as well as any conduct or statements made in negotiation thereof, is inadmissible to prove the invalidity of the claim or any part of it.[1]

1155. Evidence that a person was, at the time a harm was suffered by another, insured wholly or partially against loss arising from liability for that harm is inadmissible to prove negligence or other wrongdoing.[1]

1156. (a) In-hospital medical or medical-dental staff committees of a licensed hospital may engage in research and medical or dental study for the purpose of reducing morbidity or mortality, and may make findings and recommendations relating to such purpose. Except as provided in subdivision (b), the written records of interviews, reports, statements, or memoranda of such in-hospital medical or medical-dental staff committees relating to such medical or dental studies are subject to Title 4 (commencing with Section 2016.010) of Part 4 of the Code of Civil Procedure (relating to discovery proceedings) but, subject to subdivisions (c) and (d), shall not be admitted as evidence in any action or before any administrative body, agency, or person.

(b) The disclosure, with or without the consent of the patient, of information concerning him to such in-hospital medical or medical-dental staff committee does not make unprivileged any information that would otherwise be privileged under Section 994 or 1014; but, notwithstanding Sections 994 and 1014, such information is subject to discovery under subdivision (a) except that the identity of any patient may not be discovered under subdivision (a) unless the patient consents to such disclosure.

(c) This section does not affect the admissibility in evidence of the original medical or dental records of any patient.

(d) This section does not exclude evidence which is relevant evidence in a criminal action.[92]

1156.1. (a) A committee established in compliance with Sections 4070 and 5624 of the Welfare and Institutions Code may engage in research and medical or psychiatric study for the purpose of reducing morbidity or mortality, and may make findings and recommendations to the county and state relating to such purpose. Except as provided in subdivision (b), the written records of interviews, reports, statements, or memoranda of such committees relating to such medical or psychiatric studies are subject to Title 4 (commencing with Section 2016.010) of Part 4 of the Code of Civil Procedure but, subject to subdivisions (c) and (d), shall not be admitted as evidence in any action or before any administrative body, agency, or person.

(b) The disclosure, with or without the consent of the patient, of information concerning him or her to such committee does not make unprivileged any information that would otherwise be privileged under Section 994 or 1014. However, notwithstanding Sections 994 and 1014, such information is subject to discovery under subdivision (a) except that the identity of any patient may not be discovered under subdivision (a) unless the patient consents to such disclosure.

(c) This section does not affect the admissibility in evidence of the original medical or psychiatric records of any patient.

(d) This section does not exclude evidence which is relevant evidence in a criminal action.[93]

1156.5. (a) Evidence that a person suffered or experienced excited delirium shall not be admitted in any civil action.

(b) A party or witness may describe the factual circumstances surrounding the case, including a person's demeanor, conduct, and physical and mental condition at issue, including, but not limited to, a person's state of agitation, excitability, paranoia, extreme aggression, physical violence, and apparent immunity to pain, but shall not describe or diagnose such demeanor, conduct, or condition by use of the term excited delirium, or attribute such demeanor, conduct, or physical and mental condition to that term.

(c) For the purposes of this section, "excited delirium" means a term used to describe a person's state of agitation, excitability, paranoia, extreme aggression, physical violence, and apparent immunity to pain that is not listed in the most current version of the Diagnostic and Statistical Manual of Mental Disorders, or for which the court finds there is insufficient scientific evidence or diagnostic criteria to be recognized as a medical condition. Excited delirium also includes excited delirium syndrome, excited delirium, hyperactive delirium, agitated delirium, and exhaustive mania.[173]

1157. (a) Neither the proceedings nor the records of organized committees of medical, medical-dental, podiatric, registered dietitian, psychological, marriage and family therapist, licensed clinical social worker, professional clinical counselor, pharmacist, prehospital emergency medical care person or personnel, or veterinary staffs, or of a peer review body, as defined in Section 805 of the Business and Professions Code, having the responsibility of evaluation and improvement of the quality of care rendered in the hospital, or for that peer review body, or medical or dental review or dental hygienist review or chiropractic review or podiatric review or registered dietitian review or pharmacist review or veterinary review or acupuncturist review or licensed midwife review or prehospital emergency medical care person or personnel review committees of local medical, dental, dental hygienist, podiatric, dietetic, pharmacist, veterinary, acupuncture, chiropractic, or prehospital emergency medical care person or personnel societies, marriage and family therapist, licensed clinical social worker, professional clinical counselor, or psychological review committees of state or local marriage and family therapist, state or local licensed clinical social worker, state or local licensed professional clinical counselor, or state or local psychological associations or societies or licensed midwife associations or societies having the responsibility of evaluation and improvement of the quality of care, shall be subject to discovery.

(b) Except as hereinafter provided, a person in attendance at a meeting of any of the committees described in subdivision (a) shall not be required to testify as to what transpired at that meeting.

(c) The prohibition relating to discovery or testimony does not apply to the statements made by a person in attendance at a meeting of any of the committees described in subdivision (a) if that person is a party to an action or proceeding the subject matter of which was reviewed at that meeting, to a person requesting hospital staff privileges, or in an action against an insurance carrier alleging bad faith by the carrier in refusing to accept a settlement offer within the policy limits.

(d) The prohibitions in this section do not apply to medical, dental, dental hygienist, podiatric, dietetic, psychological, marriage and family therapist, licensed clinical social worker, professional clinical counselor, pharmacist, veterinary, acupuncture, midwifery, chiropractic, or prehospital emergency medical care person or personnel society committees that exceed 10 percent of the membership of the society, nor to any of those committees if a person serves upon the committee when his or her own conduct or practice is being reviewed.

(e) The amendments made to this section by Chapter 1081 of the Statutes of 1983, or at the 1985 portion of the 1985-86 Regular Session of the Legislature, at the 1990 portion of the 1989-90 Regular Session of the Legislature, at the 2000 portion of the 1999-2000 Regular Session of the Legislature, at the 2011 portion of the 2011-12 Regular Session of the Legislature, at the 2015 portion of the 2015-16 Regular Session of the Legislature, or at the 2024 portion of the 2023-24 Regular Session of the Legislature, do not exclude the discovery or use of relevant evidence in a criminal action.

(f) For purposes of this section, "prehospital emergency medical care person or personnel" has the same meaning as defined in paragraph (1) of subdivision (a) of Section 1797.188 of the Health and Safety Code.[174]

1157.5. Except in actions involving a claim of a provider of health care services for payment for such services, the prohibition relating to discovery or testimony provided by Section 1157 shall be applicable to the proceedings or records of an organized committee of any nonprofit medical care foundation or professional standards review organization which is organized in a manner which makes available professional competence to review health care services with respect to medical necessity, quality of care, or economic justification of charges or level of care.[23]

1157.6. Neither the proceedings nor the records of a committee established in compliance with Sections 4070 and 5624 of the Welfare and Institutions Code having the responsibility of evaluation and improvement of the quality of mental health care rendered in county operated and contracted mental health facilities shall be subject to discovery. Except as provided in this section, no person in attendance at a meeting of any such committee shall be required to testify as to what transpired thereat. The prohibition relating to discovery or testimony shall not apply to the statements made by any person in attendance at such a meeting who is a party to an action or proceeding the subject matter of which was reviewed at such meeting, or to any person requesting facility staff privileges.[25]

1157.7. The prohibition relating to discovery or testimony provided in Section 1157 shall be applicable to proceedings and records of any committee established by a local governmental agency to monitor, evaluate, and report on the necessity, quality, and level of specialty health services, including, but not limited to, trauma care services, provided by a general acute care hospital that has been designated or recognized by that governmental agency as qualified to render specialty health care services. The provisions of Division 10 (commencing with Section 7920.000) of Title 1 of the Government Code and Chapter 9 (commencing with Section 54950) of Division 2 of Title 5 of the Government Code shall not be applicable to the committee records and proceedings.[161]

1158. (a) For purposes of this section, "medical provider" means physician and surgeon, dentist, registered nurse, dispensing optician, registered physical therapist, podiatrist, licensed psychologist, osteopathic physician and surgeon, chiropractor, clinical laboratory bioanalyst, clinical laboratory technologist, or pharmacist or pharmacy, duly licensed as such under the laws of the state, or a licensed hospital.
(b) Before the filing of any action or the appearance of a defendant in an action, if an attorney at law or his or her representative presents a written authorization therefor signed by an adult patient, by the guardian or conservator of his or her person or estate, or, in the case of a minor, by a parent or guardian of the minor, or by the personal representative or an heir of a deceased patient, or a copy thereof, to a medical provider, the medical provider shall promptly make all of the patient's records under the medical provider's custody or control available for inspection and copying by the attorney at law or his or her representative.
(c) Copying of medical records shall not be performed by a medical provider, or by an agent thereof, when the requesting attorney has employed a professional photocopier or anyone identified in Section 22451 of the Business and Professions Code as his or

her representative to obtain or review the records on his or her behalf. The presentation of the authorization by the agent on behalf of the attorney shall be sufficient proof that the agent is the attorney's representative.

(d) Failure to make the records available during business hours, within five days after the presentation of the written authorization, may subject the medical provider having custody or control of the records to liability for all reasonable expenses, including attorney's fees, incurred in any proceeding to enforce this section.

(e) (1) All reasonable costs incurred by a medical provider in making patient records available pursuant to this section may be charged against the attorney who requested the records.

(2) "Reasonable cost," as used in this section, shall include, but not be limited to, the following specific costs: ten cents ($0.10) per page for standard reproduction of documents of a size 81/2 by 14 inches or less; twenty cents ($0.20) per page for copying of documents from microfilm; actual costs for the reproduction of oversize documents or the reproduction of documents requiring special processing which are made in response to an authorization; reasonable clerical costs incurred in locating and making the records available to be billed at the maximum rate of sixteen dollars ($16) per hour per person, computed on the basis of four dollars ($4) per quarter hour or fraction thereof; actual postage charges; and actual costs, if any, charged to the witness by a third person for the retrieval and return of records held by that third person.

(f) If the records are delivered to the attorney or the attorney's representative for inspection or photocopying at the record custodian's place of business, the only fee for complying with the authorization shall not exceed fifteen dollars ($15), plus actual costs, if any, charged to the record custodian by a third person for retrieval and return of records held offsite by the third person.

(g) If the records requested pursuant to subdivision (b) are maintained electronically and if the requesting party requests an electronic copy of such information, the medical provider shall provide the requested medical records in the electronic form and format requested by the requesting party, if it is readily producible in such form and format, or, if not, in a readable form and format as agreed to by the medical provider and the requesting party.

(h) A medical provider shall accept a signed and completed authorization form for the disclosure of health information if both of the following conditions are satisfied:

(1) The medical provider determines that the form is valid.

(2) The form is printed in a typeface no smaller than 14-point type and is in substantially the following form:

AUTHORIZATION FOR DISCLOSURE OF HEALTH INFORMATION PURSUANT TO EVIDENCE CODE SECTION 1158
The undersigned authorizes the medical provider designated below to disclose specified medical records to a designated recipient. The medical provider shall not condition treatment, payment, enrollment, or eligibility for benefits on the submission of this authorization.

Medical provider: ________________

Patient name: ________________
Medical record number: ________________
Date of birth: ________________
Address: ________________
Telephone number: ________________
Email: ________________

Recipient name: ________________
Recipient address: ________________
Recipient telephone number: ________________
Recipient email: ________________

Health information requested (check all that apply):
___Records dated from ________ to ________.
___Radiology records: ________ images or films ________ reports________digital/CD, if available.
___Laboratory results dated.
___Laboratory results regarding specific test(s) only (specify)________.
___All records.
___Records related to a specific injury, treatment, or other purpose (specify): ________________.

Note: records may include information related to mental health, alcohol or drug use, and HIV or AIDS. However, treatment records from mental health and alcohol or drug departments and results of HIV tests will not be disclosed unless specifically requested (check all that apply):

___Mental health records.
___Alcohol or drug records.
___HIV test results.

Method of delivery of requested records:
___Mail

___Pick up
___Electronic delivery, recipient email:________________

This authorization is effective for one year from the date of the signature unless a different date is specified here: ________________.

This authorization may be revoked upon written request, but any revocation will not apply to information disclosed before receipt of the written request.

A copy of this authorization is as valid as the original. The undersigned has the right to receive a copy of this authorization.

Notice: Once the requested health information is disclosed, any disclosure of the information by the recipient may no longer be protected under the federal Health Insurance Portability and Accountability Act of 1996 (HIPAA).

Patient signature*: ________________
Date: ________________
Print name: ________________

*If not signed by the patient, please indicate relationship to the patient (check one, if applicable):

___Parent or guardian of minor patient who could not have consented to health care.
___Guardian or conservator of an incompetent patient.
___Beneficiary or personal representative of deceased patient.[125]

1159. (a) No evidence pertaining to live animal experimentation, including, but not limited to, injury, impact, or crash experimentation, shall be admissible in any product liability action involving a motor vehicle or vehicles.
(b) This section shall apply to cases for which a trial has not actually commenced, as described in paragraph (6) of subdivision (a) of Section 581 of the Code of Civil Procedure, on January 1, 1993.[51]

1160. (a) The portion of statements, writings, or benevolent gestures expressing sympathy or a general sense of benevolence relating to the pain, suffering, or death of a person involved in an accident and made to that person or to the family of that person shall be inadmissible as evidence of an admission of liability in a civil action. A statement of fault, however, which is part of, or in addition to, any of the above shall not be inadmissible pursuant to this section.
(b) For purposes of this section:
(1) "Accident" means an occurrence resulting in injury or death to one or more persons which is not the result of willful action by a party.
(2) "Benevolent gestures" means actions which convey a sense of compassion or commiseration emanating from humane impulses.
(3) "Family" means the spouse, parent, grandparent, stepmother, stepfather, child, grandchild, brother, sister, half brother, half sister, adopted children of parent, or spouse's parents of an injured party.[73]

1161. (a) Evidence that a victim of human trafficking, as defined in Section 236.1 of the Penal Code, has engaged in any commercial sexual act as a result of being a victim of human trafficking is inadmissible to prove the victim's criminal liability for the commercial sexual act.
(b) Evidence of sexual history or history of any commercial sexual act of a victim of human trafficking, as defined in Section 236.1 of the Penal Code, is inadmissible to attack the credibility or impeach the character of the victim in any civil or criminal proceeding.[120]
Note: This section was added on Nov. 6, 2012, by initiative Prop. 35.

1162. Evidence that a victim of, or a witness to, a serious felony as defined in subdivision (c) of Section 1192.7 of, an assault in violation of subdivision (a) of Section 245 of, domestic violence in violation of Section 273.5 of, extortion in violation of Section 518 of, human trafficking in violation of Section 236.1 of, sexual battery in violation of subdivision (a) of Section 243.4 of, or stalking in violation of Section 646.9 of, the Penal Code, has engaged in an act of prostitution at or around the time they were the victim of or witness to the crime is inadmissible in a separate prosecution of that victim or witness to prove criminal liability for the act of prostitution.[150]

DIVISION 10: HEARSAY EVIDENCE

DIVISION 10 ENACTED BY STATS. 1965, CH. 299.
SECTION 1200 - 1390

Chapter 1: General Provisions

Chapter 1 enacted by Stats. 1965, Ch. 299.

1200. (a) "Hearsay evidence" is evidence of a statement that was made other than by a witness while testifying at the hearing and that is offered to prove the truth of the matter stated.
(b) Except as provided by law, hearsay evidence is inadmissible.
(c) This section shall be known and may be cited as the hearsay rule.[1]

1201. A statement within the scope of an exception to the hearsay rule is not inadmissible on the ground that the evidence of such statement is hearsay evidence if such hearsay evidence consists of one or more statements each of which meets the requirements of an exception to the hearsay rule.[4]

1202. Evidence of a statement or other conduct by a declarant that is inconsistent with a statement by such declarant received in evidence as hearsay evidence is not inadmissible for the purpose of attacking the credibility of the declarant though he is not given and has not had an opportunity to explain or to deny such inconsistent statement or other conduct. Any other evidence offered to attack or support the credibility of the declarant is admissible if it would have been admissible had the declarant been a witness at the hearing. For the purposes of this section, the deponent of a deposition taken in the action in which it is offered shall be deemed to be a hearsay declarant.[1]

1203. (a) The declarant of a statement that is admitted as hearsay evidence may be called and examined by any adverse party as if under cross-examination concerning the statement.
(b) This section is not applicable if the declarant is (1) a party, (2) a person identified with a party within the meaning of subdivision (d) of Section 776, or (3) a witness who has testified in the action concerning the subject matter of the statement.
(c) This section is not applicable if the statement is one described in Article 1 (commencing with Section 1220), Article 3 (commencing with Section 1235), or Article 10 (commencing with Section 1300) of Chapter 2 of this division.
(d) A statement that is otherwise admissible as hearsay evidence is not made inadmissible by this section because the declarant who made the statement is unavailable for examination pursuant to this section.[1]

1203.1. Section 1203 is not applicable if the hearsay statement is offered at a preliminary examination, as provided in Section 872 of the Penal Code.[45]
Note: Prop. 115 is titled the Crime Victims Justice Reform Act.

1204. A statement that is otherwise admissible as hearsay evidence is inadmissible against the defendant in a criminal action if the statement was made, either by the defendant or by another, under such circumstances that it is inadmissible against the defendant under the Constitution of the United States or the State of California.[1]

1205. Nothing in this division shall be construed to repeal by implication any other statute relating to hearsay evidence.[1]

Chapter 2: Exceptions to the Hearsay Rule

Chapter 2 enacted by Stats. 1965, Ch. 299.

Article 1: Confessions and Admissions
Article 1 enacted by Stats. 1965, Ch. 299.

1220. Evidence of a statement is not made inadmissible by the hearsay rule when offered against the declarant in an action to which he is a party in either his individual or representative capacity, regardless of whether the statement was made in his individual or representative capacity.[1]

1221. Evidence of a statement offered against a party is not made inadmissible by the hearsay rule if the statement is one of which the party, with knowledge of the content thereof, has by words or other conduct manifested his adoption or his belief in its truth.[1]

1222. Evidence of a statement offered against a party is not made inadmissible by the hearsay rule if:
(a) The statement was made by a person authorized by the party to make a statement or statements for him concerning the subject matter of the statement; and
(b) The evidence is offered either after admission of evidence sufficient to sustain a finding of such authority or, in the court's discretion as to the order of proof, subject to the admission of such evidence.[1]

1223. Evidence of a statement offered against a party is not made inadmissible by the hearsay rule if:
(a) The statement was made by the declarant while participating in a conspiracy to commit a crime or civil wrong and in furtherance of the objective of that conspiracy;
(b) The statement was made prior to or during the time that the party was participating in that conspiracy; and
(c) The evidence is offered either after admission of evidence sufficient to sustain a finding of the facts specified in subdivisions (a) and (b) or, in the court's discretion as to the order of proof, subject to the admission of such evidence.[1]

1224. When the liability obligation, or duty of a party to a civil action is based in whole or in part upon the liability, obligation, or duty of the declarant, or when the claim or right asserted by a party to a civil action is barred or diminished by a breach of duty by the declarant, evidence of a statement made by the declarant is as admissible against the party as it would be if offered against the declarant in an action involving that liability, obligation, duty, or breach of duty.[1]

1225. When a right, title, or interest in any property or claim asserted by a party to a civil action requires a determination that a right, title, or interest exists or existed in the declarant, evidence of a statement made by the declarant during the time the party now claims the declarant was the holder of the right, title, or interest is as admissible against the party as it would be if offered against the declarant in an action involving that right, title, or interest.[1]

1226. Evidence of a statement by a minor child is not made inadmissible by the hearsay rule if offered against the plaintiff in an action brought under Section 376 of the Code of Civil Procedure for injury to such minor child.[1]

1227. Evidence of a statement by the deceased is not made inadmissible by the hearsay rule if offered against the plaintiff in an action for wrongful death brought under Article 6 (commencing with Section 377.60) of Chapter 4 of Title 3 of Part 2 of the Code of Civil Procedure.[170]

1228. Notwithstanding any other provision of law, for the purpose of establishing the elements of the crime in order to admit as evidence the confession of a person accused of violating Section 261, 264.1, 285, 286, 287, 288, 289, or 647a of, or former Section 288a of, the Penal Code, a court, in its discretion, may determine that a statement of the complaining witness is not made inadmissible by the hearsay rule if it finds all of the following:
(a) The statement was made by a minor child under the age of 12, and the contents of the statement were included in a written report of a law enforcement official or an employee of a county welfare department.
(b) The statement describes the minor child as a victim of sexual abuse.
(c) The statement was made prior to the defendant's confession. The court shall view with caution the testimony of a person recounting hearsay where there is evidence of personal bias or prejudice.
(d) There are no circumstances, such as significant inconsistencies between the confession and the statement concerning material facts establishing any element of the crime or the identification of the defendant, that would render the statement unreliable.
(e) The minor child is found to be unavailable pursuant to paragraph (2) or (3) of subdivision (a) of Section 240 or refuses to testify.
(f) The confession was memorialized in a trustworthy fashion by a law enforcement official.
If the prosecution intends to offer a statement of the complaining witness pursuant to this section, the prosecution shall serve a written notice upon the defendant at least 10 days prior to the hearing or trial at which the prosecution intends to offer the statement.
If the statement is offered during trial, the court's determination shall be made out of the presence of the jury. If the statement is found to be admissible pursuant to this section, it shall be admitted out of the presence of the jury and solely for the purpose of determining the admissibility of the confession of the defendant.[148]

1228.1. (a) Except as provided in subdivision (b), neither the signature of any parent or legal guardian on a child welfare services case plan nor the acceptance of any services prescribed in the child welfare services case plan by any parent or legal guardian shall constitute an admission of guilt or be used as evidence against the parent or legal guardian in a court of law.
(b) A parent's or guardian's failure to cooperate, except for good cause, in the provision of services specified in the child welfare services case plan may be used as evidence, if relevant, in any hearing held pursuant to Section 366.21, 366.22, or 388 of the Welfare and Institutions Code and at any jurisdictional or dispositional hearing held

on a petition filed pursuant to Section 300, 342, or 387 of the Welfare and Institutions Code.[68]

Article 2: Declarations Against Interest
Article 2 enacted by Stats. 1965, Ch. 299.

1230. Evidence of a statement by a declarant having sufficient knowledge of the subject is not made inadmissible by the hearsay rule if the declarant is unavailable as a witness and the statement, when made, was so far contrary to the declarant's pecuniary or proprietary interest, or so far subjected him to the risk of civil or criminal liability, or so far tended to render invalid a claim by him against another, or created such a risk of making him an object of hatred, ridicule, or social disgrace in the community, that a reasonable man in his position would not have made the statement unless he believed it to be true.[1]

Article 2.5: Sworn Statements Regarding Gang-Related Crimes
Article 2.5 added by Stats. 1997, Ch. 499, Sec. 1.

1231. Evidence of a prior statement made by a declarant is not made inadmissible by the hearsay rule if the declarant is deceased and the proponent of introducing the statement establishes each of the following:
(a) The statement relates to acts or events relevant to a criminal prosecution under provisions of the California Street Terrorism Enforcement and Prevention Act (Chapter 11 (commencing with Section 186.20) of Title 7 of Part 1 of the Penal Code).
(b) A verbatim transcript, copy, or record of the statement exists. A record may include a statement preserved by means of an audio or video recording or equivalent technology.
(c) The statement relates to acts or events within the personal knowledge of the declarant.
(d) The statement was made under oath or affirmation in an affidavit; or was made at a deposition, preliminary hearing, grand jury hearing, or other proceeding in compliance with law, and was made under penalty of perjury.
(e) The declarant died from other than natural causes.
(f) The statement was made under circumstances that would indicate its trustworthiness and render the declarant's statement particularly worthy of belief. For purposes of this subdivision, circumstances relevant to the issue of trustworthiness include, but are not limited to, all of the following:
(1) Whether the statement was made in contemplation of a pending or anticipated criminal or civil matter, in which the declarant had an interest, other than as a witness.
(2) Whether the declarant had a bias or motive for fabricating the statement, and the extent of any bias or motive.
(3) Whether the statement is corroborated by evidence other than statements that are admissible only pursuant to this section.
(4) Whether the statement was a statement against the declarant's interest.[66]

1231.1. A statement is admissible pursuant to Section 1231 only if the proponent of the statement makes known to the adverse party the intention to offer the statement and the particulars of the statement sufficiently in advance of the proceedings to provide the adverse party with a fair opportunity to prepare to meet the statement.[66]

1231.2. A peace officer may administer and certify oaths for purposes of this article.[71]

1231.3. Any law enforcement officer testifying as to any hearsay statement pursuant to this article shall either have five years of law enforcement experience or have completed a training course certified by the Commission on Peace Officer Standards and Training which includes training in the investigation and reporting of cases and testifying at preliminary hearings and trials.[66]

1231.4. If evidence of a prior statement is introduced pursuant to this article, the jury may not be told that the declarant died from other than natural causes, but shall merely be told that the declarant is unavailable.[66]

Article 3: Prior Statements of Witnesses
Article 3 enacted by Stats. 1965, Ch. 299.

1235. Evidence of a statement made by a witness is not made inadmissible by the hearsay rule if the statement is inconsistent with his testimony at the hearing and is offered in compliance with Section 770.[1]

1236. Evidence of a statement previously made by a witness is not made inadmissible by the hearsay rule if the statement is consistent with his testimony at the hearing and is offered in compliance with Section 791.[1]

1237. (a) Evidence of a statement previously made by a witness is not made inadmissible by the hearsay rule if the statement would have been admissible if made by him while testifying, the statement concerns a matter as to which the witness has insufficient present recollection to enable him to testify fully and accurately, and the statement is contained in a writing which:

(1) Was made at a time when the fact recorded in the writing actually occurred or was fresh in the witness' memory;

(2) Was made (i) by the witness himself or under his direction or (ii) by some other person for the purpose of recording the witness' statement at the time it was made;

(3) Is offered after the witness testifies that the statement he made was a true statement of such fact; and

(4) Is offered after the writing is authenticated as an accurate record of the statement.

(b) The writing may be read into evidence, but the writing itself may not be received in evidence unless offered by an adverse party.[1]

1238. Evidence of a statement previously made by a witness is not made inadmissible by the hearsay rule if the statement would have been admissible if made by him while testifying and:

(a) The statement is an identification of a party or another as a person who participated in a crime or other occurrence;

(b) The statement was made at a time when the crime or other occurrence was fresh in the witness' memory; and

(c) The evidence of the statement is offered after the witness testifies that he made the identification and that it was a true reflection of his opinion at that time.[1]

Article 4: Spontaneous, Contemporaneous, and Dying Declarations
Article 4 enacted by Stats. 1965, Ch. 299.

1240. Evidence of a statement is not made inadmissible by the hearsay rule if the statement:
(a) Purports to narrate, describe, or explain an act, condition, or event perceived by the declarant; and
(b) Was made spontaneously while the declarant was under the stress of excitement caused by such perception.[1]

1241. Evidence of a statement is not made inadmissible by the hearsay rule if the statement:
(a) Is offered to explain, qualify, or make understandable conduct of the declarant; and
(b) Was made while the declarant was engaged in such conduct.[1]

1242. Evidence of a statement made by a dying person respecting the cause and circumstances of his death is not made inadmissible by the hearsay rule if the statement was made upon his personal knowledge and under a sense of immediately impending death.[1]

Article 5: Statements of Mental or Physical State
Article 5 enacted by Stats. 1965, Ch. 299.

1250. (a) Subject to Section 1252, evidence of a statement of the declarant's then existing state of mind, emotion, or physical sensation (including a statement of intent, plan, motive, design, mental feeling, pain, or bodily health) is not made inadmissible by the hearsay rule when:
(1) The evidence is offered to prove the declarant's state of mind, emotion, or physical sensation at that time or at any other time when it is itself an issue in the action; or
(2) The evidence is offered to prove or explain acts or conduct of the declarant.
(b) This section does not make admissible evidence of a statement of memory or belief to prove the fact remembered or believed.[1]

1251. Subject to Section 1252, evidence of a statement of the declarant's state of mind, emotion, or physical sensation (including a statement of intent, plan, motive, design, mental feeling, pain, or bodily health) at a time prior to the statement is not made inadmissible by the hearsay rule if:
(a) The declarant is unavailable as a witness; and
(b) The evidence is offered to prove such prior state of mind, emotion, or physical sensation when it is itself an issue in the action and the evidence is not offered to prove any fact other than such state of mind, emotion, or physical sensation.[1]

1252. Evidence of a statement is inadmissible under this article if the statement was made under circumstances such as to indicate its lack of trustworthiness.[1]

1253. Subject to Section 1252, evidence of a statement is not made inadmissible by the hearsay rule if the statement was made for purposes of medical diagnosis or treatment and describes medical history, or past or present symptoms, pain, or sensations, or the inception or general character of the cause or external source thereof insofar as reasonably pertinent to diagnosis or treatment. This section applies only to a statement made by a victim who is a minor at the time of the proceedings, provided the statement was made when the victim was under the age of 12 describing any act, or attempted act, of child abuse or neglect. "Child abuse" and "child neglect," for purposes of this section, have the meanings provided in subdivision (c) of Section 1360. In addition, "child abuse" means any act proscribed by Chapter 5 (commencing with Section 281) of Title 9 of Part 1 of the Penal Code committed against a minor.[58]

Article 6: Statements Relating to Wills and to Claims Against Estates
Article 6 enacted by Stats. 1965, Ch. 299.

1260. (a) Except as provided in subdivision (b), evidence of any of the following statements made by a declarant who is unavailable as a witness is not made inadmissible by the hearsay rule:
(1) That the declarant has or has not made a will or established or amended a revocable trust.
(2) That the declarant has or has not revoked his or her will, revocable trust, or an amendment to a revocable trust.
(3) That identifies the declarant's will, revocable trust, or an amendment to a revocable trust.
(b) Evidence of a statement is inadmissible under this section if the statement was made under circumstances that indicate its lack of trustworthiness.[107]

1261. (a) Evidence of a statement is not made inadmissible by the hearsay rule when offered in an action upon a claim or demand against the estate of the declarant if the statement was made upon the personal knowledge of the declarant at a time when the matter had been recently perceived by him and while his recollection was clear.
(b) Evidence of a statement is inadmissible under this section if the statement was made under circumstances such as to indicate its lack of trustworthiness.[1]

Article 7: Business Records
Article 7 enacted by Stats. 1965, Ch. 299.

1270. As used in this article, "a business" includes every kind of business, governmental activity, profession, occupation, calling, or operation of institutions, whether carried on for profit or not.[1]

1271. Evidence of a writing made as a record of an act, condition, or event is not made inadmissible by the hearsay rule when offered to prove the act, condition, or event if:
(a) The writing was made in the regular course of a business;
(b) The writing was made at or near the time of the act, condition, or event;
(c) The custodian or other qualified witness testifies to its identity and the mode of its preparation; and
(d) The sources of information and method and time of preparation were such as to indicate its trustworthiness.[1]

1272. Evidence of the absence from the records of a business of a record of an asserted act, condition, or event is not made inadmissible by the hearsay rule when offered to prove the nonoccurrence of the act or event, or the nonexistence of the condition, if:
(a) It was the regular course of that business to make records of all such acts, conditions, or events at or near the time of the act, condition, or event and to preserve them; and
(b) The sources of information and method and time of preparation of the records of that business were such that

the absence of a record of an act, condition, or event is a trustworthy indication that the act or event did not occur or the condition did not exist.[1]

Article 8: Official Records and Other Official Writings
Article 8 enacted by Stats. 1965, Ch. 299.

1280. Evidence of a writing made as a record of an act, condition, or event is not made inadmissible by the hearsay rule when offered in any civil or criminal proceeding to prove the act, condition, or event if all of the following applies:
(a) The writing was made by and within the scope of duty of a public employee.
(b) The writing was made at or near the time of the act, condition, or event.
(c) The sources of information and method and time of preparation were such as to indicate its trustworthiness.[64]

1281. Evidence of a writing made as a record of a birth, fetal death, death, or marriage is not made inadmissible by the hearsay rule if the maker was required by law to file the writing in a designated public office and the writing was made and filed as required by law.[1]

1282. A written finding of presumed death made by an employee of the United States authorized to make such finding pursuant to the Federal Missing Persons Act (56 Stats. 143, 1092, and P.L. 408, Ch. 371, 2d Sess. 78th Cong.; 50 U.S.C. App. 1001-1016), as enacted or as heretofore or hereafter amended, shall be received in any court, office, or other place in this state as evidence of the death of the person therein found to be dead and of the date, circumstances, and place of his disappearance.[1]

1283. An official written report or record that a person is missing, missing in action, interned in a foreign country, captured by a hostile force, beleaguered by a hostile force, besieged by a hostile force, or detained in a foreign country against his will, or is dead or is alive, made by an employee of the United States authorized by any law of the United States to make such report or record shall be received in any court, office, or other place in this state as evidence that such person is missing, missing in action, interned in a foreign country, captured by a hostile force, beleaguered by a hostile force, besieged by a hostile force, or detained in a foreign country against his will, or is dead or is alive.[1]

1284. Evidence of a writing made by the public employee who is the official custodian of the records in a public office, reciting diligent search and failure to find a record, is not made inadmissible by the hearsay rule when offered to prove the absence of a record in that office.[1]

1285. Within an official written report or record of a law enforcement officer regarding a sexual offense that resulted in a person's conviction, the following statements are not made inadmissible by the hearsay rule at the civil hearing described in Section 6602 of the Welfare and Institutions Code when offered to prove the truth of the matter stated:
(a) A statement from a victim of the sexual offense.
(b) A statement from an eyewitness to the sexual offense.

(c) A statement from a sexual assault medical examiner who examined a victim of the sexual offense.[172]

Article 9: Former Testimony

Article 9 enacted by Stats. 1965, Ch. 299.

1290. As used in this article, "former testimony" means testimony given under oath in:
(a) Another action or in a former hearing or trial of the same action;
(b) A proceeding to determine a controversy conducted by or under the supervision of an agency that has the power to determine such a controversy and is an agency of the United States or a public entity in the United States;
(c) A deposition taken in compliance with law in another action; or
(d) An arbitration proceeding if the evidence of such former testimony is a verbatim transcript thereof.[1]

1291. (a) Evidence of former testimony is not made inadmissible by the hearsay rule if the declarant is unavailable as a witness and:
(1) The former testimony is offered against a person who offered it in evidence in his own behalf on the former occasion or against the successor in interest of such person; or
(2) The party against whom the former testimony is offered was a party to the action or proceeding in which the testimony was given and had the right and opportunity to cross-examine the declarant with an interest and motive similar to that which he has at the hearing.
(b) The admissibility of former testimony under this section is subject to the same limitations and objections as though the declarant were testifying at the hearing, except that former testimony offered under this section is not subject to:
(1) Objections to the form of the question which were not made at the time the former testimony was given.
(2) Objections based on competency or privilege which did not exist at the time the former testimony was given.[1]

1292. (a) Evidence of former testimony is not made inadmissible by the hearsay rule if:
(1) The declarant is unavailable as a witness;
(2) The former testimony is offered in a civil action; and
(3) The issue is such that the party to the action or proceeding in which the former testimony was given had the right and opportunity to cross-examine the declarant with an interest and motive similar to that which the party against whom the testimony is offered has at the hearing.
(b) The admissibility of former testimony under this section is subject to the same limitations and objections as though the declarant were testifying at the hearing, except that former testimony offered under this section is not subject to objections based on competency or privilege which did not exist at the time the former testimony was given.[1]

1293. (a) Evidence of former testimony made at a preliminary examination by a minor child who was the complaining witness is not made inadmissible by the hearsay rule if:
(1) The former testimony is offered in a proceeding to declare the minor a dependent child of the court pursuant to Section 300 of the Welfare and Institutions Code.

(2) The issues are such that a defendant in the preliminary examination in which the former testimony was given had the right and opportunity to cross-examine the minor child with an interest and motive similar to that which the parent or guardian against whom the testimony is offered has at the proceeding to declare the minor a dependent child of the court.

(b) The admissibility of former testimony under this section is subject to the same limitations and objections as though the minor child were testifying at the proceeding to declare him or her a dependent child of the court.

(c) The attorney for the parent or guardian against whom the former testimony is offered or, if none, the parent or guardian may make a motion to challenge the admissibility of the former testimony upon a showing that new substantially different issues are present in the proceeding to declare the minor a dependent child than were present in the preliminary examination.

(d) As used in this section, "complaining witness" means the alleged victim of the crime for which a preliminary examination was held.

(e) This section shall apply only to testimony made at a preliminary examination on and after January 1, 1990.[42]

1294. (a) The following evidence of prior inconsistent statements of a witness properly admitted in a conditional examination, preliminary hearing, or trial of the same criminal matter pursuant to Section 1235 is not made inadmissible by the hearsay rule if the witness is unavailable and former testimony of the witness is admitted pursuant to Section 1291:

(1) A video or audio recorded statement introduced at a conditional examination, preliminary hearing, or prior proceeding concerning the same criminal matter.

(2) A transcript, containing the statements, of the conditional examination, preliminary hearing, or prior proceeding concerning the same criminal matter.

(b) The party against whom the prior inconsistent statements are offered, at his or her option, may examine or cross-examine any person who testified at the conditional examination, preliminary hearing, or prior proceeding, as to the prior inconsistent statements of the witness.

(c) As used in this section, "conditional examination" has the same meaning as in Chapter 4 (commencing with Section 1335) of Title 10 of Part 2 of the Penal Code.[141]

Article 10: Judgments

Article 10 enacted by Stats. 1965, Ch. 299.

1300. Evidence of a final judgment adjudging a person guilty of a crime punishable as a felony is not made inadmissible by the hearsay rule when offered in a civil action to prove any fact essential to the judgment whether or not the judgment was based on a plea of nolo contendere.[27]

1301. Evidence of a final judgment is not made inadmissible by the hearsay rule when offered by the judgment debtor to prove any fact which was essential to the judgment in an action in which he seeks to:

(a) Recover partial or total indemnity or exoneration for money paid or liability incurred because of the judgment;

(b) Enforce a warranty to protect the judgment debtor against the liability determined by the judgment; or
(c) Recover damages for breach of warranty substantially the same as the warranty determined by the judgment to have been breached.[1]

1302. When the liability, obligation, or duty of a third person is in issue in a civil action, evidence of a final judgment against that person is not made inadmissible by the hearsay rule when offered to prove such liability, obligation, or duty.[1]

Article 11: Family History
Article 11 enacted by Stats. 1965, Ch. 299.

1310. (a) Subject to subdivision (b), evidence of a statement by a declarant who is unavailable as a witness concerning his own birth, marriage, divorce, a parent and child relationship, relationship by blood or marriage, race, ancestry, or other similar fact of his family history is not made inadmissible by the hearsay rule, even though the declarant had no means of acquiring personal knowledge of the matter declared.
(b) Evidence of a statement is inadmissible under this section if the statement was made under circumstances such as to indicate its lack of trustworthiness.[16]

1311. (a) Subject to subdivision (b), evidence of a statement concerning the birth, marriage, divorce, death, parent and child relationship, race, ancestry, relationship by blood or marriage, or other similar fact of the family history of a person other than the declarant is not made inadmissible by the hearsay rule if the declarant is unavailable as a witness and:
(1) The declarant was related to the other by blood or marriage; or
(2) The declarant was otherwise so intimately associated with the other's family as to be likely to have had accurate information concerning the matter declared and made the statement (i) upon information received from the other or from a person related by blood or marriage to the other or (ii) upon repute in the other's family.
(b) Evidence of a statement is inadmissible under this section if the statement was made under circumstances such as to indicate its lack of trustworthiness.[16]

1312. Evidence of entries in family Bibles or other family books or charts, engravings on rings, family portraits, engravings on urns, crypts, or tombstones, and the like, is not made inadmissible by the hearsay rule when offered to prove the birth, marriage, divorce, death, parent and child relationship, race, ancestry, relationship by blood or marriage, or other similar fact of the family history of a member of the family by blood or marriage.[16]

1313. Evidence of reputation among members of a family is not made inadmissible by the hearsay rule if the reputation concerns the birth, marriage, divorce, death, parent and child relationship, race, ancestry, relationship by blood or marriage, or other similar fact of the family history of a member of the family by blood or marriage.[16]

1314. Evidence of reputation in a community concerning the date or fact of birth, marriage, divorce, or death of a person resident in the community at the time of the reputation is not made inadmissible by the hearsay rule.[1]

1315. Evidence of a statement concerning a person's birth, marriage, divorce, death, parent and child relationship, race, ancestry, relationship by blood or marriage, or other similar fact of family history which is contained in a writing made as a record of a church, religious denomination, or religious society is not made inadmissible by the hearsay rule if:
(a) The statement is contained in a writing made as a record of an act, condition, or event that would be admissible as evidence of such act, condition, or event under Section 1271; and
(b) The statement is of a kind customarily recorded in connection with the act, condition, or event recorded in the writing.[16]

1316. Evidence of a statement concerning a person's birth, marriage, divorce, death, parent and child relationship, race, ancestry, relationship by blood or marriage, or other similar fact of family history is not made inadmissible by the hearsay rule if the statement is contained in a certificate that the maker thereof performed a marriage or other ceremony or administered a sacrament and:
(a) The maker was a clergyman, civil officer, or other person authorized to perform the acts reported in the certificate by law or by the rules, regulations, or requirements of a church, religious denomination, or religious society; and
(b) The certificate was issued by the maker at the time and place of the ceremony or sacrament or within a reasonable time thereafter.[16]

Article 12: Reputation and Statements Concerning Community History, Property Interests, and Character

Article 12 enacted by Stats. 1965, Ch. 299.

1320. Evidence of reputation in a community is not made inadmissible by the hearsay rule if the reputation concerns an event of general history of the community or of the state or nation of which the community is a part and the event was of importance to the community.[1]

1321. Evidence of reputation in a community is not made inadmissible by the hearsay rule if the reputation concerns the interest of the public in property in the community and the reputation arose before controversy.[1]

1322. Evidence of reputation in a community is not made inadmissible by the hearsay rule if the reputation concerns boundaries of, or customs affecting, land in the community and the reputation arose before controversy.[1]

1323. Evidence of a statement concerning the boundary of land is not made inadmissible by the hearsay rule if the declarant is unavailable as a witness and had sufficient knowledge of the subject, but evidence of a statement is not admissible under this section if the statement was made under circumstances such as to indicate its lack of trustworthiness.[1]

1324. Evidence of a person's general reputation with reference to his character or a trait of his character at a relevant time in the community in which he then resided or in a group with which he then habitually associated is not made inadmissible by the hearsay rule.[1]

Article 13: Dispositive Instruments and Ancient Writings
Article 13 enacted by Stats. 1965, Ch. 299.

1330. Evidence of a statement contained in a deed of conveyance or a will or other writing purporting to affect an interest in real or personal property is not made inadmissible by the hearsay rule if:
(a) The matter stated was relevant to the purpose of the writing;
(b) The matter stated would be relevant to an issue as to an interest in the property; and
(c) The dealings with the property since the statement was made have not been inconsistent with the truth of the statement.[1]

1331. Evidence of a statement is not made inadmissible by the hearsay rule if the statement is contained in a writing more than 30 years old and the statement has been since generally acted upon as true by persons having an interest in the matter.[1]

Article 14: Commercial, Scientific, and Similar Publications
Article 14 enacted by Stats. 1965, Ch. 299.

1340. Evidence of a statement, other than an opinion, contained in a tabulation, list, directory, register, or other published compilation is not made inadmissible by the hearsay rule if the compilation is generally used and relied upon as accurate in the course of a business as defined in Section 1270.[1]

1341. Historical works, books of science or art, and published maps or charts, made by persons indifferent between the parties, are not made inadmissible by the hearsay rule when offered to prove facts of general notoriety and interest.[1]

Article 15: Declarant Unavailable as Witness
Article 15 added by Stats. 1985, Ch. 783, Sec. 1.

1350. (a) In a criminal proceeding charging a serious felony, evidence of a statement made by a declarant is not made inadmissible by the hearsay rule if the declarant is unavailable as a witness, and all of the following are true:
(1) There is clear and convincing evidence that the declarant's unavailability was knowingly caused by, aided by, or solicited by the party against whom the statement is offered for the purpose of preventing the arrest or prosecution of the party and is the result of the death by homicide or the kidnapping of the declarant.
(2) There is no evidence that the unavailability of the declarant was caused by, aided by, solicited by, or procured on behalf of, the party who is offering the statement.
(3) The statement has been memorialized in a tape recording made by a law enforcement official, or in a written statement prepared by a law enforcement official and signed by the declarant and notarized in the presence of the law enforcement official, prior to the death or kidnapping of the declarant.
(4) The statement was made under circumstances which indicate its trustworthiness and was not the result of promise, inducement, threat, or coercion.
(5) The statement is relevant to the issues to be tried.
(6) The statement is corroborated by other evidence which tends to connect

the party against whom the statement is offered with the commission of the serious felony with which the party is charged. The corroboration is not sufficient if it merely shows the commission of the offense or the circumstances thereof.

(b) If the prosecution intends to offer a statement pursuant to this section, the prosecution shall serve a written notice upon the defendant at least 10 days prior to the hearing or trial at which the prosecution intends to offer the statement, unless the prosecution shows good cause for the failure to provide that notice. In the event that good cause is shown, the defendant shall be entitled to a reasonable continuance of the hearing or trial.

(c) If the statement is offered during trial, the court's determination shall be made out of the presence of the jury. If the defendant elects to testify at the hearing on a motion brought pursuant to this section, the court shall exclude from the examination every person except the clerk, the court reporter, the bailiff, the prosecutor, the investigating officer, the defendant and his or her counsel, an investigator for the defendant, and the officer having custody of the defendant. Notwithstanding any other provision of law, the defendant's testimony at the hearing shall not be admissible in any other proceeding except the hearing brought on the motion pursuant to this section. If a transcript is made of the defendant's testimony, it shall be sealed and transmitted to the clerk of the court in which the action is pending.

(d) As used in this section, "serious felony" means any of the felonies listed in subdivision (c) of Section 1192.7 of the Penal Code or any violation of Section 11351, 11352, 11378, or 11379 of the Health and Safety Code.

(e) If a statement to be admitted pursuant to this section includes hearsay statements made by anyone other than the declarant who is unavailable pursuant to subdivision (a), those hearsay statements are inadmissible unless they meet the requirements of an exception to the hearsay rule.[77]

Article 16: Statements by Children Under the Age of 12 in Child Neglect and Abuse Proceedings

Article 16 added by Stats. 1995, Ch. 87, Sec. 3.

1360. (a) In a criminal prosecution where the victim is a minor, a statement made by the victim when under the age of 12 describing any act of child abuse or neglect performed with or on the child by another, or describing any attempted act of child abuse or neglect with or on the child by another, is not made inadmissible by the hearsay rule if all of the following apply:

(1) The statement is not otherwise admissible by statute or court rule.

(2) The court finds, in a hearing conducted outside the presence of the jury, that the time, content, and circumstances of the statement provide sufficient indicia of reliability.

(3) The child either:

(A) Testifies at the proceedings.

(B) Is unavailable as a witness, in which case the statement may be admitted only if there is evidence of the child abuse or neglect that corroborates the statement made by the child.

(b) A statement may not be admitted under this section unless the proponent of the statement makes known to the adverse party the intention to offer the statement and the particulars of the statement sufficiently in advance of the proceedings in order to provide the adverse party with a fair opportunity to prepare to meet the statement.

(c) For purposes of this section, "child abuse" means an act proscribed by Section 273a, 273d, or 288.5 of the Penal Code, or any of the acts described in Section 11165.1 of the Penal Code, and "child neglect" means any of the acts described in Section 11165.2 of the Penal Code.[59]

Article 17: Physical Abuse
Article 17 added by Stats. 1996, Ch. 416, Sec. 2.

1370. (a) Evidence of a statement by a declarant is not made inadmissible by the hearsay rule if all of the following conditions are met:

(1) The statement purports to narrate, describe, or explain the infliction or threat of physical injury upon the declarant.

(2) The declarant is unavailable as a witness pursuant to Section 240.

(3) The statement was made at or near the time of the infliction or threat of physical injury. Evidence of statements made more than five years before the filing of the current action or proceeding shall be inadmissible under this section.

(4) The statement was made under circumstances that would indicate its trustworthiness.

(5) The statement was made in writing, was electronically recorded, or made to a physician, nurse, paramedic, or to a law enforcement official.

(b) For purposes of paragraph (4) of subdivision (a), circumstances relevant to the issue of trustworthiness include, but are not limited to, the following:

(1) Whether the statement was made in contemplation of pending or anticipated litigation in which the declarant was interested.

(2) Whether the declarant has a bias or motive for fabricating the statement, and the extent of any bias or motive.

(3) Whether the statement is corroborated by evidence other than statements that are admissible only pursuant to this section.

(c) A statement is admissible pursuant to this section only if the proponent of the statement makes known to the adverse party the intention to offer the statement and the particulars of the statement sufficiently in advance of the proceedings in order to provide the adverse party with a fair opportunity to prepare to meet the statement.[75]

1380. (a) In a criminal proceeding charging a violation, or attempted violation, of Section 368 of the Penal Code, evidence of a statement made by a declarant is not made inadmissible by the hearsay rule if the declarant is unavailable as a witness, as defined in subdivisions (a) and (b) of Section 240, and all of the following are true:

(1) The party offering the statement has made a showing of particularized guarantees of trustworthiness regarding the statement, the statement was made under circumstances which indicate its trustworthiness, and the statement was not the result of promise, inducement, threat, or coercion. In making its determination, the court may consider only the circumstances that surround the making of the statement and that render the declarant particularly worthy of belief.

(2) There is no evidence that the unavailability of the declarant was caused by, aided by, solicited by, or procured on behalf of, the party who is offering the statement.

(3) The entire statement has been memorialized in a videotape recording made by a law enforcement official, prior to the death or disabling of the declarant.

(4) The statement was made by the victim of the alleged violation.

(5) The statement is supported by corroborative evidence.

(6) The victim of the alleged violation is an individual who meets both of the following requirements:

(A) Was 65 years of age or older or was a dependent adult when the alleged violation or attempted violation occurred.

(B) At the time of any criminal proceeding, including, but not limited to, a preliminary hearing or trial, regarding the alleged violation or attempted violation, is either deceased or suffers from the infirmities of aging as manifested by advanced age or organic brain damage, or other physical, mental, or emotional dysfunction, to the extent that the ability of the person to provide adequately for the person's own care or protection is impaired.

(b) If the prosecution intends to offer a statement pursuant to this section, the prosecution shall serve a written notice upon the defendant at least 10 days prior to the hearing or trial at which the prosecution intends to offer the statement, unless the prosecution shows good cause for the failure to provide that notice. In the event that good cause is shown, the defendant shall be entitled to a reasonable continuance of the hearing or trial.

(c) If the statement is offered during trial, the court's determination as to the availability of the victim as a witness shall be made out of the presence of the jury. If the defendant elects to testify at the hearing on a motion brought pursuant to this section, the court shall exclude from the examination every person except the clerk, the court reporter, the bailiff, the prosecutor, the investigating officer, the defendant and his or her counsel, an investigator for the defendant, and the officer having custody of the defendant. Notwithstanding any other provision of law, the defendant's testimony at the hearing shall not be admissible in any other proceeding except the hearing brought on the motion pursuant to this section. If a transcript is made of the defendant's testimony, it shall be sealed and transmitted to the clerk of the court in which the action is pending.[72]

1390. (a) Evidence of a statement is not made inadmissible by the hearsay rule if the statement is offered against a party that has engaged, or aided and abetted, in the wrongdoing that was intended to, and did, procure the unavailability of the declarant as a witness.

(b) (1) The party seeking to introduce a statement pursuant to subdivision (a) shall establish, by a preponderance of the evidence, that the elements of subdivision (a) have been met at a foundational hearing.

(2) The hearsay evidence that is the subject of the foundational hearing is admissible at the foundational hearing. However, a finding that the elements of subdivision (a) have been met shall not be based solely on the

unconfronted hearsay statement of the unavailable declarant, and shall be supported by independent corroborative evidence.

(3) The foundational hearing shall be conducted outside the presence of the jury. However, if the hearing is conducted after a jury trial has begun, the judge presiding at the hearing may consider evidence already presented to the jury in deciding whether the elements of subdivision (a) have been met.

(4) In deciding whether or not to admit the statement, the judge may take into account whether it is trustworthy and reliable.

(c) This section shall apply to any civil, criminal, or juvenile case or proceeding initiated or pending as of January 1, 2011.[124]

DIVISION 11: WRITINGS

DIVISION 11 ENACTED BY STATS. 1965, CH. 299.
SECTION 1400 - 1605

Chapter 1: Authentication and Proof of Writings

Chapter 1 enacted by Stats. 1965, Ch. 299.

Article 1: Requirement of Authentication

Article 1 enacted by Stats. 1965, Ch. 299.

1400. Authentication of a writing means (a) the introduction of evidence sufficient to sustain a finding that it is the writing that the proponent of the evidence claims it is or (b) the establishment of such facts by any other means provided by law.[1]

1401. (a) Authentication of a writing is required before it may be received in evidence.
(b) Authentication of a writing is required before secondary evidence of its content may be received in evidence.[1]

1402. The party producing a writing as genuine which has been altered, or appears to have been altered, after its execution, in a part material to the question in dispute, must account for the alteration or appearance thereof. He may show that the alteration was made by another, without his concurrence, or was made with the consent of the parties affected by it, or otherwise properly or innocently made, or that the alteration did not change the meaning or language of the instrument. If he does that, he may give the writing in evidence, but not otherwise.[1]

Article 2: Means of Authenticating and Proving Writings

Article 2 enacted by Stats. 1965, Ch. 299.

1410. Nothing in this article shall be construed to limit the means by which a writing may be authenticated or proved.[1]

1410.5. (a) For purposes of this chapter, a writing shall include any graffiti consisting of written words, insignia, symbols, or any other markings which convey a particular meaning.
(b) Any writing described in subdivision (a), or any photograph thereof, may be admitted into evidence in an action for vandalism, for the purpose of proving that the writing was made by the defendant.
(c) The admissibility of any fact offered to prove that the writing was made by the defendant shall, upon motion of the defendant, be ruled upon outside the presence of the jury, and is subject to the requirements of Sections 1416, 1417, and 1418.[43]

1411. Except as provided by statute, the testimony of a subscribing witness is not required to authenticate a writing.[1]

1412. If the testimony of a subscribing witness is required by statute to authenticate a writing and the subscribing witness denies or does not recollect the execution of the writing, the writing may be authenticated by other evidence.[1]

1413. A writing may be authenticated

by anyone who saw the writing made or executed, including a subscribing witness.[1]

1414. A writing may be authenticated by evidence that:
(a) The party against whom it is offered has at any time admitted its authenticity; or
(b) The writing has been acted upon as authentic by the party against whom it is offered.[1]

1415. A writing may be authenticated by evidence of the genuineness of the handwriting of the maker.[1]

1416. A witness who is not otherwise qualified to testify as an expert may state his opinion whether a writing is in the handwriting of a supposed writer if the court finds that he has personal knowledge of the handwriting of the supposed writer. Such personal knowledge may be acquired from:
(a) Having seen the supposed writer write;
(b) Having seen a writing purporting to be in the handwriting of the supposed writer and upon which the supposed writer has acted or been charged;
(c) Having received letters in the due course of mail purporting to be from the supposed writer in response to letters duly addressed and mailed by him to the supposed writer; or
(d) Any other means of obtaining personal knowledge of the handwriting of the supposed writer.[1]

1417. The genuineness of handwriting, or the lack thereof, may be proved by a comparison made by the trier of fact with handwriting (a) which the court finds was admitted or treated as genuine by the party against whom the evidence is offered or (b) otherwise proved to be genuine to the satisfaction of the court.[1]

1418. The genuineness of writing, or the lack thereof, may be proved by a comparison made by an expert witness with writing (a) which the court finds was admitted or treated as genuine by the party against whom the evidence is offered or (b) otherwise proved to be genuine to the satisfaction of the court.[1]

1419. Where a writing whose genuineness is sought to be proved is more than 30 years old, the comparison under Section 1417 or 1418 may be made with writing purporting to be genuine, and generally respected and acted upon as such, by persons having an interest in knowing whether it is genuine.[1]

1420. A writing may be authenticated by evidence that the writing was received in response to a communication sent to the person who is claimed by the proponent of the evidence to be the author of the writing.[1]

1421. A writing may be authenticated by evidence that the writing refers to or states matters that are unlikely to be known to anyone other than the person who is claimed by the proponent of the evidence to be the author of the writing.[1]

Article 3: Presumptions Affecting Acknowledged Writings and Official Writings
Article 3 enacted by Stats. 1965, Ch. 299.

1450. The presumptions established by this article are presumptions affecting the burden of producing evidence.[1]

1451. A certificate of the acknowledgment of a writing other than a will, or a certificate of the proof of such a writing, is prima facie evidence of the facts recited in the certificate and the genuineness of the signature of each person by whom the writing purports to have been signed if the certificate meets the requirements of Article 3 (commencing with Section 1180) of Chapter 4, Title 4, Part 4, Division 2 of the Civil Code.[1]

1452. A seal is presumed to be genuine and its use authorized if it purports to be the seal of:
(a) The United States or a department, agency, or public employee of the United States.
(b) A public entity in the United States or a department, agency, or public employee of such public entity.
(c) A nation recognized by the executive power of the United States or a department, agency, or officer of such nation.
(d) A public entity in a nation recognized by the executive power of the United States or a department, agency, or officer of such public entity.
(e) A court of admiralty or maritime jurisdiction.
(f) A notary public within any state of the United States.[1]

1453. A signature is presumed to be genuine and authorized if it purports to be the signature, affixed in his official capacity, of:
(a) A public employee of the United States.
(b) A public employee of any public entity in the United States.
(c) A notary public within any state of the United States.[1]

1454. A signature is presumed to be genuine and authorized if it purports to be the signature, affixed in his official capacity, of an officer, or deputy of an officer, of a nation or public entity in a nation recognized by the executive power of the United States and the writing to which the signature is affixed is accompanied by a final statement certifying the genuineness of the signature and the official position of (a) the person who executed the writing or (b) any foreign official who has certified either the genuineness of the signature and official position of the person executing the writing or the genuineness of the signature and official position of another foreign official who has executed a similar certificate in a chain of such certificates beginning with a certificate of the genuineness of the signature and official position of the person executing the writing. The final statement may be made only by a secretary of an embassy or legation, consul general, consul, vice consul, consular agent, or other officer in the foreign service of the United States stationed in the nation, authenticated by the seal of his office.[1]

Chapter 2: Secondary Evidence of Writings

Chapter 2 enacted by Stats. 1965, Ch. 299.

Article 1: Proof of the Content of a Writing

Article 1 repealed and added by Stats. 1998, Ch. 100, Sec. 2.

1520. The content of a writing may be proved by an otherwise admissible original.[70]

1521. (a) The content of a writing may be proved by otherwise admissible secondary evidence. The court shall exclude secondary evidence of the content of writing if the court determines either of the following:

(1) A genuine dispute exists concerning material terms of the writing and justice requires the exclusion.

(2) Admission of the secondary evidence would be unfair.

(b) Nothing in this section makes admissible oral testimony to prove the content of a writing if the testimony is inadmissible under Section 1523 (oral testimony of the content of a writing).

(c) Nothing in this section excuses compliance with Section 1401 (authentication).

(d) This section shall be known as the "Secondary Evidence Rule."[70]

1522. (a) In addition to the grounds for exclusion authorized by Section 1521, in a criminal action the court shall exclude secondary evidence of the content of a writing if the court determines that the original is in the proponent's possession, custody, or control, and the proponent has not made the original reasonably available for inspection at or before trial. This section does not apply to any of the following:

(1) A duplicate as defined in Section 260.

(2) A writing that is not closely related to the controlling issues in the action.

(3) A copy of a writing in the custody of a public entity.

(4) A copy of a writing that is recorded in the public records, if the record or a certified copy of it is made evidence of the writing by statute.

(b) In a criminal action, a request to exclude secondary evidence of the content of a writing, under this section or any other law, shall not be made in the presence of the jury.[70]

1523. (a) Except as otherwise provided by statute, oral testimony is not admissible to prove the content of a writing.

(b) Oral testimony of the content of a writing is not made inadmissible by subdivision (a) if the proponent does not have possession or control of a copy of the writing and the original is lost or has been destroyed without fraudulent intent on the part of the proponent of the evidence.

(c) Oral testimony of the content of a writing is not made inadmissible by subdivision (a) if the proponent does not have possession or control of the original or a copy of the writing and either of the following conditions is satisfied:

(1) Neither the writing nor a copy of the writing was reasonably procurable by the proponent by use of the court's process or by other available means.

(2) The writing is not closely related to the controlling issues and it would be inexpedient to require its production.

(d) Oral testimony of the content of a writing is not made inadmissible by subdivision (a) if the writing consists of numerous accounts or other writings that cannot be examined in court without great loss of time, and the evidence sought from them is only the general result of the whole.[70]

Article 2: Official Writings and Recorded Writings
Article 2 enacted by Stats. 1965, Ch. 299.

1530. (a) A purported copy of a writing in the custody of a public entity, or of an entry in such a writing, is prima facie evidence of the existence and content of such writing or entry if:

(1) The copy purports to be published by the authority of the nation or state, or public entity therein in which the

writing is kept;

(2) The office in which the writing is kept is within the United States or within the Panama Canal Zone, the Trust Territory of the Pacific Islands, or the Ryukyu Islands, and the copy is attested or certified as a correct copy of the writing or entry by a public employee, or a deputy of a public employee, having the legal custody of the writing; or

(3) The office in which the writing is kept is not within the United States or any other place described in paragraph (2) and the copy is attested as a correct copy of the writing or entry by a person having authority to make attestation. The attestation must be accompanied by a final statement certifying the genuineness of the signature and the official position of (i) the person who attested the copy as a correct copy or (ii) any foreign official who has certified either the genuineness of the signature and official position of the person attesting the copy or the genuineness of the signature and official position of another foreign official who has executed a similar certificate in a chain of such certificates beginning with a certificate of the genuineness of the signature and official position of the person attesting the copy. Except as provided in the next sentence, the final statement may be made only by a secretary of an embassy or legation, consul general, consul, vice consul, or consular agent of the United States, or a diplomatic or consular official of the foreign country assigned or accredited to the United States. Prior to January 1, 1971, the final statement may also be made by a secretary of an embassy or legation, consul general, consul, vice consul, consular agent, or other officer in the foreign service of the United States stationed in the nation in which the writing is kept, authenticated by the seal of his office. If reasonable opportunity has been given to all parties to investigate the authenticity and accuracy of the documents, the court may, for good cause shown, (i) admit an attested copy without the final statement or (ii) permit the writing or entry in foreign custody to be evidenced by an attested summary with or without a final statement.

(b) The presumptions established by this section are presumptions affecting the burden of producing evidence.[8]

1531. For the purpose of evidence, whenever a copy of a writing is attested or certified, the attestation or certificate must state in substance that the copy is a correct copy of the original, or of a specified part thereof, as the case may be.[1]

1532. (a) The official record of a writing is prima facie evidence of the existence and content of the original recorded writing if:

(1) The record is in fact a record of an office of a public entity; and

(2) A statute authorized such a writing to be recorded in that office.

(b) The presumption established by this section is a presumption affecting the burden of producing evidence.[1]

Article 3: Photographic Copies and Printed Representations of Writings

Heading of Article 3 amended by Stats. 1998, Ch. 100, Sec. 3.

1550. (a) If made and preserved as a part of the records of a business, as defined in Section 1270, in the regular course of that business, the following types of evidence of a writing are as admissible as the writing itself:

(1) A nonerasable optical image reproduction or any other reproduction of a public record by a trusted system, as defined in Section 12168.7 of the Government Code, if additions, deletions, or changes to the original document are not permitted by the technology.

(2) A photostatic copy or reproduction.

(3) A microfilm, microcard, or miniature photographic copy, reprint, or enlargement.

(4) Any other photographic copy or reproduction, or an enlargement thereof.

(b) The introduction of evidence of a writing pursuant to subdivision (a) does not preclude admission of the original writing if it is still in existence. A court may require the introduction of a hard copy printout of the document.[79]

1550.1. Reproductions of files, records, writings, photographs, fingerprints or other instruments in the official custody of a criminal justice agency that were microphotographed or otherwise reproduced in a manner that conforms with the provisions of Section 11106.1, 11106.2, or 11106.3 of the Penal Code shall be admissible to the same extent and under the same circumstances as the original file, record, writing or other instrument would be admissible.[90]

1551. A print, whether enlarged or not, from a photographic film (including a photographic plate, microphotographic film, photostatic negative, or similar reproduction) of an original writing destroyed or lost after such film was taken or a reproduction from an electronic recording of video images on magnetic surfaces is admissible as the original writing itself if, at the time of the taking of such film or electronic recording, the person under whose direction and control it was taken attached thereto, or to the sealed container in which it was placed and has been kept, or incorporated in the film or electronic recording, a certification complying with the provisions of Section 1531 and stating the date on which, and the fact that, it was so taken under his direction and control.[6]

1552. (a) A printed representation of computer information or a computer program is presumed to be an accurate representation of the computer information or computer program that it purports to represent. This presumption is a presumption affecting the burden of producing evidence. If a party to an action introduces evidence that a printed representation of computer information or computer program is inaccurate or unreliable, the party introducing the printed representation into evidence has the burden of proving, by a preponderance of evidence, that the printed representation is an accurate representation of the existence and content of the computer information or computer program that it purports to represent.

(b) Subdivision (a) applies to the printed representation of computer-generated information st-ored by an automated traffic enforcement system.

(c) Subdivision (a) shall not apply to computer-generated official records certified in accordance with Section 452.5 or 1530.[116]

1553. (a) A printed representation of

images stored on a video or digital medium is presumed to be an accurate representation of the images it purports to represent. This presumption is a presumption affecting the burden of producing evidence. If a party to an action introduces evidence that a printed representation of images stored on a video or digital medium is inaccurate or unreliable, the party introducing the printed representation into evidence has the burden of proving, by a preponderance of evidence, that the printed representation is an accurate representation of the existence and content of the images that it purports to represent.

(b) Subdivision (a) applies to the printed representation of video or photographic images stored by an automated traffic enforcement system.[117]

Article 4: Production of Business Records
Heading of Article 4 amended by Stats. 1969, Ch. 199.

1560. (a) As used in this article:

(1) "Business" includes every kind of business described in Section 1270.

(2) "Record" includes every kind of record maintained by a business.

(b) Except as provided in Section 1564, when a subpoena duces tecum is served upon the custodian of records or other qualified witness of a business in an action in which the business is neither a party nor the place where any cause of action is alleged to have arisen, and the subpoena requires the production of all or any part of the records of the business, it is sufficient compliance therewith if the custodian or other qualified witness delivers by mail or otherwise a true, legible, and durable copy of all of the records described in the subpoena to the clerk of the court or to another person described in subdivision (d) of Section 2026.010 of the Code of Civil Procedure, together with the affidavit described in Section 1561, within one of the following time periods:

(1) In any criminal action, five days after the receipt of the subpoena.

(2) In any civil action, within 15 days after the receipt of the subpoena.

(3) Within the time agreed upon by the party who served the subpoena and the custodian or other qualified witness.

(c) The copy of the records shall be separately enclosed in an inner envelope or wrapper, sealed, with the title and number of the action, name of witness, and date of subpoena clearly inscribed thereon; the sealed envelope or wrapper shall then be enclosed in an outer envelope or wrapper, sealed, and directed as follows:

(1) If the subpoena directs attendance in court, to the clerk of the court.

(2) If the subpoena directs attendance at a deposition, to the officer before whom the deposition is to be taken, at the place designated in the subpoena for the taking of the deposition or at the officer's place of business.

(3) In other cases, to the officer, body, or tribunal conducting the hearing, at a like address.

(d) Unless the parties to the proceeding otherwise agree, or unless the sealed envelope or wrapper is returned to a witness who is to appear personally, the copy of the records shall remain sealed and shall be opened only at the time of trial, deposition, or other hearing, upon the direction of the judge, officer, body, or tribunal conducting the proceeding, in the presence of all parties who have appeared in person or by counsel at the trial, deposition, or hearing. Records that are original documents and that are not introduced in evidence or required as part of the record shall be returned to the person or entity from whom received. Records that are copies may be destroyed.

(e) As an alternative to the procedures described in subdivisions (b), (c), and (d), the subpoenaing party in a civil action may direct the witness to make the records available for inspection or copying by the party's attorney, the attorney's representative, or deposition officer as described in Section 2020.420 of the Code of Civil Procedure, at the witness' business address under reasonable conditions during normal business hours. Normal business hours, as used in this subdivision, means those hours that the business of the witness is normally open for business to the public. When provided with at least five business days' advance notice by the party's attorney, attorney's representative, or deposition officer, the witness shall designate a time period of not less than six continuous hours on a date certain for copying of records subject to the subpoena by the party's attorney, attorney's representative, or deposition officer. It shall be the responsibility of the attorney's representative to deliver any copy of the records as directed in the subpoena. Disobedience to the deposition subpoena issued pursuant to this subdivision is punishable as provided in Section 2020.240 of the Code of Civil Procedure.

(f) If a search warrant for business records is served upon the custodian of records or other qualified witness of a business in compliance with Section 1524 of the Penal Code regarding a criminal investigation in which the business is neither a party nor the place where any crime is alleged to have occurred, and the search warrant provides that the warrant will be deemed executed if the business causes the delivery of records described in the warrant to the law enforcement agency ordered to execute the warrant, it is sufficient compliance therewith if the custodian or other qualified witness delivers by mail or otherwise a true, legible, and durable copy of all of the records described in the search warrant to the law enforcement agency ordered to execute the search warrant, together with the affidavit described in Section 1561, within five days after the receipt of the search warrant or within such other time as is set forth in the warrant. This subdivision does not abridge or limit the scope of search warrant procedures set forth in Chapter 3 (commencing with Section 1523) of Title 12 of Part 2 of the Penal Code or invalidate otherwise duly executed search warrants.[129]

1561. (a) The records shall be accompanied by the affidavit of the custodian or other qualified witness, stating in substance each of the following:

(1) The affiant is the duly authorized custodian of the records or other qualified witness and has authority to certify the records.

(2) The copy is a true copy of all the records described in the subpoena duces tecum or search warrant, or pursuant to subdivision (e) of Section 1560, the records were delivered to the attorney, the attorney's representative, or deposition officer for copying at the custodian's or witness' place of business, as the case may be.

(3) The records were prepared by the personnel of the business in the ordinary course of business at or near the time of the act, condition, or event.
(4) The identity of the records.
(5) A description of the mode of preparation of the records.

(b) If the business has none of the records described, or only part thereof, the custodian or other qualified witness shall so state in the affidavit, and deliver the affidavit and those records that are available in one of the manners provided in Section 1560.

(c) If the records described in the subpoena were delivered to the attorney or his or her representative or deposition officer for copying at the custodian's or witness' place of business, in addition to the affidavit required by subdivision (a), the records shall be accompanied by an affidavit by the attorney or his or her representative or deposition officer stating that the copy is a true copy of all the records delivered to the attorney or his or her representative or deposition officer for copying.[130]

1562. If the original records would be admissible in evidence if the custodian or other qualified witness had been present and testified to the matters stated in the affidavit, and if the requirements of Section 1271 have been met, the copy of the records is admissible in evidence. The affidavit is admissible as evidence of the matters stated therein pursuant to Section 1561 and the matters so stated are presumed true. When more than one person has knowledge of the facts, more than one affidavit may be made. The presumption established by this section is a presumption affecting the burden of producing evidence.[62]

1563. (a) This article does not require tender or payment of more than one witness fee and one mileage fee or other charge, to a witness or witness' business, unless there is an agreement to the contrary between the witness and the requesting party.

(b) All reasonable costs incurred in a civil proceeding by a witness who is not a party with respect to the production of all or any part of business records requested pursuant to a subpoena duces tecum shall be charged against the party serving the subpoena duces tecum.

(1) "Reasonable costs," as used in this section, includes, but is not limited to, the following specific costs: ten cents ($0.10) per page for standard reproduction of documents of a size 81/2 by 14 inches or less; twenty cents ($0.20) per page for copying of documents from microfilm; actual costs for the reproduction of oversize documents or the reproduction of documents requiring special processing which are made in response to a subpoena; reasonable clerical costs incurred in locating and making the records available to be billed at the maximum rate of twenty-four dollars ($24) per hour per person, computed on the basis of six dollars ($6) per quarter hour or fraction thereof; actual postage charges; and the actual cost, if any, charged to the witness by a third person for the retrieval and return of records held offsite by that third person.

(2) The requesting party, or the requesting party's deposition officer, shall not be required to pay the reasonable costs or any estimate thereof before the records are available for delivery pursuant to the subpoena,

but the witness may demand payment of costs pursuant to this section simultaneous with actual delivery of the subpoenaed records, and until payment is made, the witness is under no obligation to deliver the records.

(3) The witness shall submit an itemized statement for the costs to the requesting party, or the requesting party's deposition officer, setting forth the reproduction and clerical costs incurred by the witness. If the costs exceed those authorized in paragraph (1), or if the witness refuses to produce an itemized statement of costs as required by paragraph (3), upon demand by the requesting party, or the requesting party's deposition officer, the witness shall furnish a statement setting forth the actions taken by the witness in justification of the costs.

(4) The requesting party may petition the court in which the action is pending to recover from the witness all or a part of the costs paid to the witness, or to reduce all or a part of the costs charged by the witness, pursuant to this subdivision, on the grounds that those costs were excessive. Upon the filing of the petition the court shall issue an order to show cause and from the time the order is served on the witness the court has jurisdiction over the witness. The court may hear testimony on the order to show cause and if it finds that the costs demanded and collected, or charged but not collected, exceed the amount authorized by this subdivision, it shall order the witness to remit to the requesting party, or reduce its charge to the requesting party by an amount equal to, the amount of the excess. If the court finds the costs were excessive and charged in bad faith by the witness, the court shall order the witness to remit the full amount of the costs demanded and collected, or excuse the requesting party from any payment of costs charged but not collected, and the court shall also order the witness to pay the requesting party the amount of the reasonable expenses incurred in obtaining the order, including attorney's fees. If the court finds the costs were not excessive, the court shall order the requesting party to pay the witness the amount of the reasonable expenses incurred in defending the petition, including attorney's fees.

(5) If a subpoena is served to compel the production of business records and is subsequently withdrawn, or is quashed, modified, or limited on a motion made other than by the witness, the witness shall be entitled to reimbursement pursuant to paragraph (1) for all reasonable costs incurred in compliance with the subpoena to the time that the requesting party has notified the witness that the subpoena has been withdrawn or quashed, modified, or limited. If the subpoena is withdrawn or quashed, if those costs are not paid within 30 days after demand therefor, the witness may file a motion in the court in which the action is pending for an order requiring payment, and the court shall award the payment of expenses and attorney's fees in the manner set forth in paragraph (4).

(6) If records requested pursuant to a subpoena duces tecum are delivered to the attorney, the attorney's representative, or the deposition officer for inspection or photocopying at the witness' place of business, the only

fee for complying with the subpoena shall not exceed fifteen dollars ($15), plus the actual cost, if any, charged to the witness by a third person for retrieval and return of records held offsite by that third person. If the records are retrieved from microfilm, the reasonable costs, as defined in paragraph (1), applies.

(c) If the personal attendance of the custodian of a record or other qualified witness is required pursuant to Section 1564, in a civil proceeding, he or she shall be entitled to the same witness fees and mileage permitted in a case where the subpoena requires the witness to attend and testify before a court in which the action or proceeding is pending and to any additional costs incurred as provided by subdivision (b).[131]

1564. The personal attendance of the custodian or other qualified witness and the production of the original records is not required unless, at the discretion of the requesting party, the subpoena duces tecum contains a clause which reads:

"The personal attendance of the custodian or other qualified witness and the production of the original records are required by this subpoena. The procedure authorized pursuant to subdivision (b) of Section 1560, and Sections 1561 and 1562, of the Evidence Code will not be deemed sufficient compliance with this subpoena."[38]

1565. If more than one subpoena duces tecum is served upon the custodian of records or other qualified witness and the personal attendance of the custodian or other qualified witness is required pursuant to Section 1564, the witness shall be deemed to be the witness of the party serving the first such subpoena duces tecum.[5]

1566. This article applies in any proceeding in which testimony can be compelled.[1]

1567. A completed form described in Section 3664 of the Family Code for income and benefit information provided by the employer may be admissible in a proceeding for modification or termination of an order for child, family, or spousal support if both of the following requirements are met:

(a) The completed form complies with Sections 1561 and 1562.

(b) A copy of the completed form and notice was served on the employee named therein pursuant to Section 3664 of the Family Code.[60]

Chapter 3: Official Writings Affecting Property

Chapter 3 enacted by Stats. 1965, Ch. 299.

1600. (a) The record of an instrument or other document purporting to establish or affect an interest in property is prima facie evidence of the existence and content of the original recorded document and its execution and delivery by each person by whom it purports to have been executed if:

(1) The record is in fact a record of an office of a public entity; and

(2) A statute authorized such a document to be recorded in that office.

(b) The presumption established by this section is a presumption affecting the burden of proof.[4]

1601. (a) Subject to subdivisions (b) and (c), when in any action it is desired to prove the contents of the official record of any writing lost or destroyed by conflagration or other public calamity, after proof of such loss or destruction, the following may, without further proof, be admitted in evidence to prove the contents of such record:

(1) Any abstract of title made and issued and certified as correct prior to such loss or destruction, and purporting to have been prepared and made in the ordinary course of business by any person engaged in the business of preparing and making abstracts of title prior to such loss or destruction; or

(2) Any abstract of title, or of any instrument affecting title, made, issued, and certified as correct by any person engaged in the business of insuring titles or issuing abstracts of title to real estate, whether the same was made, issued, or certified before or after such loss or destruction and whether the same was made from the original records or from abstract and notes, or either, taken from such records in the preparation and upkeeping of its plant in the ordinary course of its business.

(b) No proof of the loss of the original writing is required other than the fact that the original is not known to the party desiring to prove its contents to be in existence.

(c) Any party desiring to use evidence admissible under this section shall give reasonable notice in writing to all other parties to the action who have appeared therein, of his intention to use such evidence at the trial of the action, and shall give all such other parties a reasonable opportunity to inspect the evidence, and also the abstracts, memoranda, or notes from which it was compiled, and to take copies thereof.[1]

1603. A deed of conveyance of real property, purporting to have been executed by a proper officer in pursuance of legal process of any of the courts of record of this state, acknowledged and recorded in the office of the recorder of the county wherein the real property therein described is situated, or the record of such deed, or a certified copy of such record, is prima facie evidence that the property or interest therein described was thereby conveyed to the grantee named in such deed. The presumption established by this section is a presumption affecting the burden of proof.[4]

1604. A certificate of purchase, or of location, of any lands in this state, issued or made in pursuance of any law of the United States or of this state, is prima facie evidence that the holder or assignee of such certificate is the owner of the land described therein; but this evidence may be overcome by proof that, at the time of the location, or time of filing a preemption claim on which the certificate may have been issued, the land was in the adverse possession of the adverse party, or those under whom he claims, or that the adverse party is holding the land for mining purposes.[1]

1605. Duplicate copies and authenticated translations of original Spanish title papers relating to land claims in this state, derived from the Spanish or Mexican governments, prepared under the supervision of the Keeper of Archives, authenticated by the Surveyor-General or his successor and by the Keeper of Archives, and filed with a county recorder, in accordance with Chapter 281 of the Statutes of 1865-66, are admissible as evidence with like force and effect as the originals and without proving the execution of such originals.[4]

ENDNOTES

[1]Enacted by Stats. 1965, Ch. 299.

[2]Added by Stats. 1965, Ch. 1151.

[3]Added by Stats. 1967, Ch. 650.

[4]Amended by Stats. 1967, Ch. 650.

[5]Amended by Stats. 1969, Ch. 199.

[6]Amended by Stats. 1969, Ch. 646.

[7]Amended by Stats. 1969, Ch. 1412.

[8]Amended by Stats. 1970, Ch. 41.

[9]Added by Stats. 1970, Ch. 69.

[10]Added by Stats. 1970, Ch. 1397.

[11]Amended by Stats. 1970, Ch. 1397.

[12]Amended by Stats. 1974, Ch. 227.

[13]Amended by Stats. 1974, Ch. 1456, Sec. 2.

[14]Amended by Stats. 1975, Ch. 71.

[15]Amended by Stats. 1975, Ch. 318.

[16]Amended by Stats. 1975, Ch. 1244.

[17]Added by Stats. 1977, Ch. 708.

[18]Added by Stats. 1978, Ch. 93.

[19]Amended by Stats. 1978, Ch. 294.

[20]Added by Stats. 1978, Ch. 528.

[21]Added by Stats. 1978, Ch. 630.

[22]Amended by Stats. 1980, Ch. 381.

[23]Amended by Stats. 1980, Ch. 524.

[24]Added by Stats. 1980, Ch. 917.

[25]Added by Stats. 1982, Ch. 234, Sec. 5. Effective June 2, 1982.

[26]Amended by Stats. 1982, Ch. 256, Sec. 2.

[27]Amended by Stats. 1982, Ch. 390, Sec. 2.

[28]Added by Stats. 1982, Ch. 1518, Sec. 2.

[29]Amended by Stats. 1983, Ch. 201, Sec. 1.

[30]Added by Stats. 1983, Ch. 202, Sec. 1. Effective July 12, 1983.

[31]Amended by Stats. 1983, Ch. 1072, Sec. 2.

[32]Amended by Stats. 1985, Ch. 884, Sec. 1.

[33]Amended by Stats. 1985, Ch. 884, Sec. 2.

[34]Added by Stats. 1985, Ch. 1328, Sec. 3.

[35]Amended by Stats. 1986, Ch. 248, Sec. 43.

[36]Added by Stats. 1986, Ch. 330, Sec. 1.

[37]Added by Stats. 1986, Ch. 854, Sec. 1.

[38]Amended by Stats. 1987, Ch. 19, Sec. 4. Effective May 12, 1987.

[39]Amended by Stats. 1987, Ch. 496, Sec. 1.

[40]Amended by Stats. 1987, Ch. 687, Sec. 1.

[41]Repealed and added by Stats. 1987, Ch. 1207, Sec. 2.

[42]Added by Stats. 1989, Ch. 322, Sec. 1.

[43]Added by Stats. 1989, Ch. 660, Sec. 1.

[44]Amended by Stats. 1989, Ch. 1359, Sec. 9.7.

[45]Added June 5, 1990, by initiative Proposition 115, Sec. 8.

[46]Amended by Stats. 1990, Ch. 295, Sec. 1.

[47]Amended by Stats. 1990, Ch. 714, Sec. 2.

[48]Added by Stats. 1990, Ch. 714, Sec. 3.

[49]Amended by Stats. 1992, Ch. 7, Sec. 4. Effective January 1, 1993.

[50]Added by Stats. 1992, Ch. 7, Sec. 5. Effective January 1, 1993.

[51]Added by Stats. 1992, Ch. 188, Sec. 1. Effective January 1, 1993.

[52]Repealed and added by Stats. 1993, Ch. 219, Sec. 77.4. Effective January 1, 1994.

[53]Added by Stats. 1994, Ch. 128, Sec. 2. Effective January 1, 1995.

[54]Amended by Stats. 1994, Ch. 1010, Sec. 103. Effective January 1, 1995.

[55]Amended by Stats. 1994, Ch. 1010, Sec. 104. Effective January 1, 1995.

[56]Amended by Stats. 1994, Ch. 1010, Sec. 105. Effective January 1, 1995.

[57]Amended by Stats. 1994, Ch. 1269, Sec. 7. Effective January 1, 1995.

[58]Added by Stats. 1995, Ch. 87, Sec. 2. Effective January 1, 1996.

[59]Added by Stats. 1995, Ch. 87, Sec. 3. Effective January 1, 1996.

[60]Added by Stats. 1995, Ch. 506, Sec. 1. Effective January 1, 1996.

[61]Amended by Stats. 1995, Ch. 938, Sec. 8. Effective January 1, 1996. Operative July 1, 1997, by Sec. 98 of Ch. 938.

[62]Amended by Stats. 1996, Ch. 146, Sec. 2. Effective January 1, 1997.

[63]Amended by Stats. 1996, Ch. 261, Sec. 1. Effective January 1, 1997.

[64]Amended by Stats. 1996, Ch. 642, Sec. 4. Effective January 1, 1997.

[65]Amended by Stats. 1997, Ch. 376, Sec. 1. Effective January 1, 1998.

[66]Added by Stats. 1997, Ch. 499, Sec. 1. Effective January 1, 1998.

[67]Added by Stats. 1997, Ch. 772, Sec. 3. Effective January 1, 1998.

[68]Amended by Stats. 1997, Ch. 793, Sec. 1. Effective January 1, 1998.

[69]Amended by Stats. 1997, Ch. 892, Sec. 11. Effective January 1, 1998.

[70]Added by Stats. 1998, Ch. 100, Sec. 2. Effective January 1, 1999.

[71]Amended by Stats. 1998, Ch. 606, Sec. 2. Effective January 1, 1999.

[72]Added by Stats. 1999, Ch. 383, Sec. 1. Effective January 1, 2000.

[73]Added by Stats. 2000, Ch. 195, Sec. 1. Effective January 1, 2001.

[74]Amended by Stats. 2000, Ch. 948, Sec. 1. Effective January 1, 2001.

[75]Amended by Stats. 2000, Ch. 1001, Sec. 2. Effective January 1, 2001.

[76]Amended by Stats. 2001, Ch. 854, Sec. 3. Effective January 1, 2002.

[77]Amended by Stats. 2001, Ch. 854, Sec. 5. Effective January 1, 2002.

[78]Amended by Stats. 2002, Ch. 72, Sec. 3. Effective January 1, 2003.

[79]Amended by Stats. 2002, Ch. 124, Sec. 1. Effective January 1, 2003. Became operative on July 9, 2012, pursuant to Stats. 2002, Ch. 124, Sec. 2.

[80]Amended by Stats. 2002, Ch. 391, Sec. 3. Effective January 1, 2003.

[81]Added by Stats. 2002, Ch. 629, Sec. 1. Effective January 1, 2003.

[82]Amended by Stats. 2002, Ch. 784, Sec. 101. Effective January 1, 2003.

[83]Amended by Stats. 2002, Ch. 784, Sec. 103. Effective January 1, 2003.

[84]Amended by Stats. 2002, Ch. 806, Sec. 19. Effective January 1, 2003.

[85]Amended by Stats. 2002, Ch. 806, Sec. 20. Effective January 1, 2003.

[86]Amended by Stats. 2002, Ch. 806, Sec. 21. Effective January 1, 2003.

[87]Amended by Stats. 2002, Ch. 806, Sec. 22. Effective January 1, 2003.

[88]Amended by Stats. 2002, Ch. 806, Sec. 23. Effective January 1, 2003.

[89]Amended by Stats. 2002, Ch. 945, Sec. 1. Effective January 1, 2003.

[90]Added by Stats. 2004, Ch. 65, Sec. 1. Effective January 1, 2005.

[91]Amended by Stats. 2004, Ch. 182, Sec. 29. Effective January 1, 2005. Operative July 1, 2005, by Sec. 64 of Ch. 182.

[92]Amended by Stats. 2004, Ch. 182, Sec. 30. Effective January 1, 2005. Operative July 1, 2005, by Sec. 64 of Ch. 182.

[93]Amended by Stats. 2004, Ch. 182, Sec. 31. Effective January 1, 2005. Operative July 1, 2005, by Sec. 64 of Ch. 182.

[94]Amended by Stats. 2004, Ch. 183, Sec. 94. Effective January 1, 2005.

[95]Amended by Stats. 2004, Ch. 823, Sec. 3. Effective January 1, 2005.

[96]Amended by Stats. 2004, Ch. 823, Sec. 4. Effective January 1, 2005.

[97]Amended by Stats. 2004, Ch. 823, Sec. 5. Effective January 1, 2005.

[98]Amended by Stats. 2005, Ch. 464, Sec. 1. Effective January 1, 2006.

[99]Amended by Stats. 2006, Ch. 689, Sec. 4. Effective January 1, 2007.

[100]Amended by Stats. 2006, Ch. 689, Sec. 6. Effective January 1, 2007.

[101]Amended by Stats. 2006, Ch. 689, Sec. 7. Effective January 1, 2007.

[102]Amended by Stats. 2007, Ch. 130, Sec. 84. Effective January 1, 2008.

[103]Amended by Stats. 2007, Ch. 206, Sec. 3. Effective January 1, 2008.

[104]Amended by Stats. 2007, Ch. 206, Sec. 4. Effective January 1, 2008.

[105]Amended by Stats. 2007, Ch. 206, Sec. 5. Effective January 1, 2008.

[106]Amended by Stats. 2009, Ch. 8, Sec. 2. (AB 1163) Effective January 1, 2010.

[107]Amended by Stats. 2010, Ch. 106, Sec. 1. (SB 1041) Effective January 1, 2011.

[108]Added by Stats. 2010, Ch. 168, Sec. 1. (AB 2195) Effective January 1, 2011.

[109]Amended by Stats. 2010, Ch. 328, Sec. 64. (SB 1330) Effective January 1, 2011.

[110]Amended by Stats. 2010, Ch. 537, Sec. 1. (AB 1723) Effective January 1, 2011.

[111]Amended by Stats. 2011, Ch. 381, Sec. 20. (SB 146) Effective January 1, 2012.

[112]Amended by Stats. 2011, Ch. 381, Sec. 22. (SB 146) Effective January 1, 2012.

[113]Amended by Stats. 2012, Ch. 470, Sec. 8. (AB 1529) Effective January 1, 2013.

[114]Amended by Stats. 2012, Ch. 470, Sec. 9. (AB 1529) Effective January 1, 2013.

[115]Amended by Stats. 2012, Ch. 470, Sec. 10. (AB 1529) Effective January 1, 2013.

[116]Amended by Stats. 2012, Ch. 735, Sec. 1. (SB 1303) Effective January 1, 2013.

[117]Amended by Stats. 2012, Ch. 735, Sec. 2. (SB 1303) Effective January 1, 2013.

[118]Amended by Stats. 2013, Ch. 19, Sec. 1. (AB 1250) Effective January 1, 2014.

[119]Added by Stats. 2013, Ch. 123, Sec. 2. (AB 267) Effective January 1, 2014.

[120]Amended by Stats. 2013, Ch. 126, Sec. 1. (AB 694) Effective January 1, 2014.

[121]Added by Stats. 2014, Ch. 685, Sec. 2. (SB 873) Effective September 27, 2014.

[122]Amended by Stats. 2014, Ch. 913, Sec. 13. (AB 2747) Effective January 1, 2015.

[123]Amended by Stats. 2015, Ch. 20, Sec. 1. (SB 79) Effective June 24, 2015.

[124]Amended by Stats. 2015, Ch. 55, Sec. 1. (AB 593) Effective January 1, 2016.

[125]Amended by Stats. 2015, Ch. 528, Sec. 1. (AB 1337) Effective January 1, 2016.

[126]Added by Stats. 2016, Ch. 50, Sec. 32. (SB 1005) Effective January 1, 2017.

[127]Amended by Stats. 2016, Ch. 50, Sec. 33. (SB 1005) Effective January 1, 2017.

[128]Amended by Stats. 2016, Ch. 50, Sec. 34. (SB 1005) Effective January 1, 2017.

[129]Amended by Stats. 2016, Ch. 85, Sec. 1. (SB 1087) Effective January 1, 2017.

[130]Amended by Stats. 2016, Ch. 85, Sec. 2. (SB 1087) Effective January 1, 2017.

[131]Amended by Stats. 2016, Ch. 85, Sec. 3. (SB 1087) Effective January 1, 2017.

[132]Amended by Stats. 2016, Ch. 94, Sec. 8. (AB 1709) Effective January 1, 2017.

[133]Added by Stats. 2016, Ch. 132, Sec. 1. (AB 2159) Effective January 1, 2017.

[134]Amended by Stats. 2017, Ch. 60, Sec. 1. (SB 217) Effective January 1, 2018.

[135]Amended by Stats. 2017, Ch. 178, Sec. 1. (SB 331) Effective January 1, 2018.

[136]Amended by Stats. 2017, Ch. 269, Sec. 1. (SB 811) Effective January 1, 2018.

[137]Amended by Stats. 2017, Ch. 434, Sec. 2. (SB 732) Effective January 1, 2018.

[138]Amended by Stats. 2017, Ch. 530, Sec. 2. (AB 1159) Effective January 1, 2018.

[139]Amended by Stats. 2017, Ch. 561, Sec. 55. (AB 1516) Effective January 1, 2018.

[140]Amended by Stats. 2017, Ch. 561, Sec. 56. (AB 1516) Effective January 1, 2018.

[141]Amended by Stats. 2018, Ch. 64, Sec. 1. (AB 1736) Effective January 1, 2019.

[142]Amended by Stats. 2018, Ch. 70, Sec. 1. (AB 1934) Effective January 1, 2019.

[143]Amended by Stats. 2018, Ch. 123, Sec. 2. (AB 1896) Effective January 1, 2019.

[144]Amended by Stats. 2018, Ch. 350, Sec. 1. (SB 954) Effective January 1, 2019.

[145]Added by Stats. 2018, Ch. 350, Sec. 2. (SB 954) Effective January 1, 2019.

[146]Amended by Stats. 2018, Ch. 423, Sec. 18. (SB 1494) Effective January 1, 2019.

[147]Amended by Stats. 2018, Ch. 423, Sec. 22. (SB 1494) Effective January 1, 2019.

[148]Amended by Stats. 2018, Ch. 423, Sec. 23. (SB 1494) Effective January 1, 2019.

[149]Amended by Stats. 2018, Ch. 475, Sec. 1. (AB 1290) Effective January 1, 2019.

[150]Amended by Stats. 2019, Ch. 141, Sec. 3. (SB 233) Effective January 1, 2020.

[151]Amended by Stats. 2019, Ch. 197, Sec. 1. (AB 1735) Effective January 1, 2020.

[152]Amended by Stats. 2019, Ch. 197, Sec. 2. (AB 1735) Effective January 1, 2020.

[153]Added by Stats. 2019, Ch. 197, Sec. 4. (AB 1735) Effective January 1, 2020.

[154]Amended by Stats. 2019, Ch. 497, Sec. 109. (AB 991) Effective January 1, 2020.

[155]Amended by Stats. 2019, Ch. 585, Sec. 2. (AB 1600) Effective January 1, 2020.

[156]Amended by Stats. 2019, Ch. 585, Sec. 3. (AB 1600) Effective January 1, 2020.

[157]Amended by Stats. 2020, Ch. 370, Sec. 113. (SB 1371) Effective January 1, 2021.

[158]Amended by Stats. 2020, Ch. 370, Sec. 114. (SB 1371) Effective January 1, 2021.

[159]Amended by Stats. 2021, Ch. 24, Sec. 1. (AB 341) Effective January 1, 2022.

[160]Amended by Stats. 2021, Ch. 402, Sec. 1. (SB 16) Effective January 1, 2022.

[161]Amended by Stats. 2021, Ch. 615, Sec. 105. (AB 474) Effective January 1, 2022. Operative January 1, 2023, pursuant to Sec. 463 of Stats. 2021, Ch. 615.

[162]Amended by Stats. 2021, Ch. 626, Sec. 7. (AB 1171) Effective January 1, 2022.

[163]Amended by Stats. 2021, Ch. 647, Sec. 74. (SB 801) Effective January 1, 2022.

[164]Added by Stats. 2022, Ch. 168, Sec. 1. (SB 836) Effective August 22, 2022.

[165]Added by Stats. 2022, Ch. 168, Sec. 2. (SB 836) Effective August 22, 2022.

[166]Amended by Stats. 2022, Ch. 86, Sec. 1. (SB 357) Effective January 1, 2023.

[167]Amended by Stats. 2022, Ch. 197, Sec. 1. (SB 1493) Effective January 1, 2023.

[168]Amended by Stats. 2022, Ch. 197, Sec. 2. (SB 1493) Effective January 1, 2023.

[169]Added by Stats. 2022, Ch. 973, Sec. 2. (AB 2799) Effective January 1, 2023.

[170]Amended by Stats. 2023, Ch. 131, Sec. 58. (AB 1754) Effective January 1, 2024.

[171]Amended (as added by Stats. 2023, Ch. 75) by Stats. 2023, Ch. 190, Sec. 1. (SB 135) Effective September 13, 2023. Operative January 1 2024, pursuant to Sec. 13 of Ch. 190, Stats 2023.

[172]Added by Stats. 2023, Ch. 363, Sec. 1. (AB 1253) Effective January 1, 2024.

[173]Added by Stats. 2023, Ch. 431, Sec. 1. (AB 360) Effective January 1, 2024.

[174]Amended by Stats. 2024, Ch. 329, Sec. 1. (AB 2225) Effective January 1, 2025.

[175]Amended by Stats. 2024, Ch. 993, Sec. 1. (SB 1386) Effective January 1, 2025.

www.ingramcontent.com/pod-product-compliance
Lightning Source LLC
LaVergne TN
LVHW021112300926
849160LV00009B/700
* 9 7 9 8 9 0 1 1 3 5 6 4 8 *